Return to Twillea Carthen
HR

Dona Latmon

THE SOUL'S MIRROR

REFLECTIONS ON THE FULLNESS OF LIFE

WRITTEN BY

Dana LaMon

PUBLISHED BY

1997

ISBN: 0-9656633-2-9

Library of Congress Catalog Number: 97-93087

ImageWorth
Post Office Box 2117
Lancaster, California 93539-2117
(805) 949-7423

Printed in the United States of America

First ImageWorth Printing: July 1997.

DEDICATION

TO MOM AND DAD, who started my life.

TO JACI, who brought fullness to my life.

TO DANA, WINTER, ANTON, AND LINNEA, who show the joy of life.

TO GOD, Who is the power of my life.

And the Lord God formed man of the dust of the ground, and breathed into his nostrils the breath of life; and man became a living soul. [Genesis 2:7]

I am come that they might have life, and that they might have it more abundantly. [John 10:10]

Pleasant words are as an honeycomb, sweet to the soul, and health to the bones. [Proverbs 16:24]

TABLE OF CONTENTS

ACKNOWLEDGMENTS

The title page of this book identifies Dana LaMon as its author. While I am responsible for the content, including any overlooked errors, it deceptively omits a number of people who were instrumental in the development and completion of this work. I devote the next two pages to acknowledge nine individuals without whose work and support this book would not be what it is.

Thank you Jacqueline Louise Jones LaMon for being a constant support and critic. From the very inception of the idea of this book to its publication, Jaci [pronounced like Jackie] encouraged me to pursue the project. She had the viewpoint as my wife to see that my life off the platform reflected the message that I present as a motivational and inspirational speaker. She traveled with me and was able to discern the reactions of the audience to the ideas that I shared. She took my advice and discovered applicability to her own life. With such three-dimensional perspective, she was the ideal person to watch the development of the book to ensure that the end product reflected the initial idea.

I appreciate Jaci's candor, offered in love, in letting me know when ideas were not clearly or fully explained. She kept reminding me of who my readers would be so that I would write to be easily understood. Because we share the same penchant for grammatical correctness, she was an excellent proofreader.

Thank you Dusty Adams for the cover design.

Thank you Harvey Harrison for your insightful

comments on the first draft and your assistance in locating a publisher.

Thank you Juanita Ingram for your pains-taking effort to ensure that The Soul's Mirror reflected no spelling or grammatical blemishes.

Thank you Dr. Peter C. Meade for offering moral and financial support for this book.

Thank you Mary Pagliaro for your vital proofreading services.

Thank you Joe Sweeney for keeping me working on the project. Joe, a mentor in the development of my professional speaking business, never failed to ask about the progress of the book each time that we talked.

Thank you Sharon White-Senghor for accepting the job as an editor. As I expected when I asked her to edit, Sharon, a Yale classmate, unhesitatingly rejected what she believed would not work for you, the reader.

Thank you Dorothy Williams for proofreading, editing, and getting the project moving when it stalled. As a professor of English, Dottie was able to offer critical comments on grammar and style. More important, however, were her words of encouragement at a point when continuation of the project was in question.

In addition to these special nine, I must thank all those people, the names of most I do not know, who talked to me after hearing me speak and asked if I had a book. Your inquiries revealed the need to put in writing what I shared from the platform.

PREFACE

On August 30, 1992, the Antelope Valley Press, a local newspaper of Lancaster, California, printed the text of the speech "Take A Chance" with which I won the World Championship of Public Speaking eight days prior. The following day, my wife answered a telephone call from a neighbor who reported that she had read the speech three times. After the first reading she was impressed and wanted to read it again. Following the second time, she thought that the message was pretty sound. Reading it the third time, she said to herself, "He is absolutely right. I must not allow comfort to stop me from finishing my education." The day that she called us to share her response to the speech she re-enrolled in college.

The greatest compliment is paid when a person tells me of the actions he or she has taken toward the fulfillment of life as a result of something I said. It pleases me to inspire and motivate others. It does not matter who is in the audience. I speak to students from elementary school to college. I speak to prison inmates and to religious congregations. I speak to those who own their businesses as well as to employees. Corporate managers and government officials benefit from my message. Why? Because they are all people, and my message is about people. About life. About the joy and success of life that all people innately long to experience.

My presentations are unique because I share my personal experiences as a blind man in a world of people who rely on sight.

On the other hand, my message is borrowed. I first heard it in church when I was quite young. It stems from the words of Jesus Christ as reported by the gospel writer John: "I am come that they might have life, and that they might have it more abundantly." [John 10:10]

Though both my Sunday school teacher and my pastor interpreted this to be a promise of bliss to be enjoyed after death, I have come to understand and believe it to be a promise of life now.

In the same passage reference is made to the "thief" who comes "to steal, and to kill, and to destroy".

I see in this Biblical passage an immutable law of the universe: EVERY LIFE IS TO BE LIFE IN ABUNDANCE SO LONG AS THE FORCES OF DESTRUCTION CAN BE RESISTED.

As I contemplated this universal law and sought to understand it in the context of the things I learned in school and in church, from reading and talking to other people, and from my experiences, I discovered two rudimentary components of the law.

> First, abundant life is a promise conferred upon one at birth. It is not something that one has to first discover and then strive during all one's time on this earth to attain.
>
> Second, the forces that steal, kill, and destroy do so from within. Words, events, or circumstances can deprive one of abundant life only by infiltrating one's mind or attacking one's soul.

Along with the understanding of the universal law of abundance was an instinctive recognition of my purpose in life: To help others to experience fulfillment in theirs. I was not certain how this purpose would be achieved, however.

Initially, it appeared that I would achieve my purpose in life through a religious ministry. When I was sixteen years old, I started speaking to my peers in youth gatherings at my church and other congregations in the Los Angeles area. I became deeply involved in the administration and ministry of the church after completing college. In 1980, I was offered the pastorship of a small congregation. Because I did not feel it to be my calling, I declined.

In 1991, I came by an unanticipated opportunity to have an impact on the lives of others. I started a business as a motivational and inspirational speaker. My decision to do so was prompted by the reaction of audiences to the speeches I delivered in contests of Toastmasters International. I perceived that people longed to be motivated and inspired to see their worth and to strive for joy and success.

Very quickly, I learned that outside of Toastmasters there was a hunger for words of encouragement and inspiration and a desire for a message of possibilities. After a while, members of the audiences began requesting tapes of my speeches. And then they wanted the message in writing.

This book is an effort to put in writing what I enjoy communicating orally. It is based on my life bccausc mc is whom I know best.

It is my belief that the ideas expressed in The Soul's Mirror can inspire you and/or provoke you to think about your life and what you are doing with it. As you take time to read, spend a moment to reflect on your own experiences.

If after reading and reflecting, your life is

enhanced, I will be pleased. The project will have been worth the effort.

If on your first look at The Soul's Mirror you see nothing applicable to you, hold on to it. Keep it in a place where you can quickly put your hands on it. As sure as you live, there will be a time when encouragement, inspiration, or motivation will help to get you back on track to fullness of life. That is what this book is for.

Dana LaMon, 1997

LOOKING IN THE SOUL'S MIRROR

This book is intended to be a reference to aid you in understanding the universal law of abundant life, the unbounded realm of possibilities, and your potential for realizing joy and success. It is designed to be a tool with which you can discover your purpose in life, unleash your potential, and maintain your motivation to achieve the desires of your heart. This reference and tool can best be used when you know its design and construction.

The Soul's Mirror contains 122 topics ranging from ABILITY to WORTH. (See the index for a complete, alphabetical list of the topics.) The one-word titles have been assigned to each segment to facilitate your finding specific words of encouragement, motivation, or inspiration when you need them most. For example: If you face tragedy, you may wish to read the topic SORROW or the topic HOPE. If you are planning to marry, you may choose to read MARRIAGE, COMMITMENT, and/or COMPROMISE. You may benefit from reading PERSEVERANCE if you are feeling discouraged because your sales calls are not netting the results you desire.

To avoid being didactic or sounding preachy, I have written the "Upon reflection" portion of each topic in the first person. The risk in doing so is the chance that I appear to be egotistical with the overuse of "I". My desire to avoid egotism is as strong as that to avoid didactic and preachy.

On the other hand, the benefit to using the

first-person voice is that the language lends itself to personal reflection. If you agree with the ideas and message of the topic and wish to adopt it as your own, it is already written in your voice. You can select specific portions as your positive affirmations.

Many pages--indeed volumes--could be written on any of the topics included here. I have chosen to write very short essays. The brevity serves two purposes. First is to accommodate a busy schedule. If you are presently traveling on the road to success or are preparing to make that journey, you are already working on a schedule that squeezes every minute out of each hour. How and where do you find the time to read a few hundred pages of a book written to motivate you? The Soul's Mirror makes the task easy by dividing the motivational material into short segments. Now you only have to find about five minutes in your daily schedule. You can get up five minutes earlier. Or you can go to bed five minutes later. Read while you sip your coffee or while on hold on the telephone. Five of the several minutes in the doctor's waiting room or at the airport can be better invested.

The second purpose for the short topics is to provide chewable chunks of motivational morsels. To obtain the greatest benefit in learning, self-improvement, and motivation you should take the information a little at a time. Consider, reflect, and process each subject before you move to the next.

Each of the 122 topics contains a cross-reference. Included in the cross-references are other topics that relate to the one that you have read. This is particularly useful if you are selecting your reading according to your need for encouragement, motiva tion, or understanding.

The 122 topics have been grouped into fifteen divisions. The categorizing is not a perfect one. For example, the topic HATRED is included with other topics on emotions, but it could also have been included in the group of "STUMBLING BLOCKS". The groupings will benefit the reader who desires to read several pieces with a related theme in one sitting.

So that The Soul's Mirror can be used as daily inspiration, a Daily Reading Calendar has been included as an appendix. If you follow this calendar, you will read through the book three times in a year. From April 7 through August 6, you will read the book in the order presented.

An index has been included to provide you with an easy reference to find the topic you need. Because it is presented alphabetically, you can quickly determine if a subject is or is not addressed in this book.

Keep The Soul's Mirror handy. At your bedside. On the coffee table. In your car. At your desk. In your purse or briefcase. Where will you be when you need a moment to reflect on your life? You could be anywhere. And everywhere that you are, you should be able to reflect on the fullness of life.

How many times have you looked into a mirror, or even a large plate-glass window, to see a reflection of yourself? We are very concerned with how we appear outwardly to others. Allow The Soul's Mirror to be your looking glass to reflect the innermost part of you. There is beauty for you to behold.

For now we see through a glass, darkly, but then face to face: now I know in part; but then shall I know even as also I am known. [I Corinthians 13:12]

THE

SOUL'S

MIRROR

REFLECTIONS ON THE FULLNESS OF LIFE

1

WHAT IS LIFE ABOUT?

Life is that segment of eternity during which my soul, mind, and body join to interact with the universe.

The sheer joy and certain success of life come from living with purpose, not by chance.

LIFE

Life is not just a bowl of cherries; it is the whole tree. Cultivate it well and you will enjoy its fruit forever.

I was born fifteen minutes after my twin sister Delora on Sunday, September 14, 1952, at 6:10 AM. My sister and I were the first two of seven children that Eddie Mae Askew and Jesse James Lamon had together. I was born black, male, but not blind. These physical characteristics were readily observed and duly noted on the certificate of live birth. What is not written is that I was also born with a mind and a soul. These, I am sure, were presumed.

Upon reflection:

I am the manifestation of the forces of nature coming together. Consisting of soul, mind, and body, I have been given life.

What is life? Life is that segment of eternity during which my soul, mind, and body join to interact with the universe. It is commonly understood as the time that I am born to the moment of my death.

How long will life be I can never know. But my body, with the instinct for survival, will seek to extend it as long as possible. My mind, on the other hand, understands that my time here is limited and, through its power of will, strives to make life as full as possible. Meanwhile, my soul, having its origin in the eternal universe, concerns itself with neither longevity nor activity. In its essence of love, the soul endeavors to experience the joy of life.

At the moment that the forces of the universe brought together the elements of my being--soul, mind, and body--they also set me on a path of life filled with joy and success. The events and experiences of my life determine whether or not I remain on course.

My view of life and attitude toward what happens to me are formed by my experiences and teaching, both formal and informal. My outlook on life may be influenced by others who themselves do not understand life. I can learn from their experiences, but I must develop my own outlook.

It is my life. It is the only one I have. I will get the most out of it by experiencing it through body, mind, and soul.

****

Reflect also on: ABUNDANCE, JOY, MIND, SOUL, SUCCESS.

ABUNDANCE

It is contentment in yourself, not the content of your things, from which life's abundance springs.

In a family of twelve children--my mother had two, my dad had three, and they married and had seven together--there were times in my childhood when bread was the only thing that I could find to eat. My siblings would butter theirs, but I did not like butter. I would sprinkle my two slices of bread with water to hold the sugar that would make my sweetened sandwich.

Years later looking at the situation, I would say we were poor. But I did not think that then. Poverty and wealth are comparative measurements of what one possesses and I had nothing with which to compare my life. Though the sugar-sandwich days were few, I had no way of knowing that they were not an ordinary occurrence which all families encountered. I had no knowledge of what others had or did not have that was different than mine. At the time, a sugar sandwich satisfied me.

Upon reflection:

I have heard the pessimistic expression "Life is not a bowl of cherries", but I refuse to adopt this cynicism as a premise of life. There are times when indeed life seems difficult, not at all cherry-like, but I believe that it is supposed to be like a bowl of cherries. My life is supposed to be a bowl of deep red, juicy, sweet cherries. I can live in abundance.

There is no end to the joy that I can experience and no limit to the successes which I can achieve.

When my bowl is not full, I go cherry picking believing that I am entitled to more. When the cherries seem to be sour, I readjust my focus and find the sweetness that is in life. When it appears that I get only the pits, I make sure that I am not letting someone else control my life.

Abundance is not a function of the volume of tangible objects I manage to amass. Those material things are immaterial when measuring the fullness of life. Neither the square footage of my living quarters nor the size of my bank account is determinative. What stock I hold or the percentage of the business that I own are not indicative of abundance. It is possible for me to own much but find little joy in what I hold.

I live in abundance when I love myself and those around me, find joy in what I do, and am satisfied that I am fulfilling my purpose in life.

****

Reflect also on: JOY, LIFE, MONEY, SUCCESS.

SUCCESS

You can find success in the journey as well as in the destination when you take the path that leads through your heart.

I have a bachelor's degree from Yale University and a law degree from the University of Southern California. I have worked continuously since completing school and have experienced an increase in my income each year. I own a business. I am happily married and enjoy my four children.

Am I successful? Yes, I am. But I do not judge my success by the degrees I hold, by my social status, or by my material possessions. Nor do I measure my success by comparing what I have to what my neighbor has. I judge myself to be successful because of what I feel inside.

Upon reflection:

The common gauges for measuring success are wealth, fame, and rank. But wealth without joy is not success. Fame without love is not success. Rank without peace is not success.

Success is more than the attainment of my goals or the achievement of my objectives. Coupled with the reaching of my ambitions must be the satisfaction of my innermost desires. I must fulfill my purpose in life. From this fulfillment will spring joy that flows into all that I do. I will have reason to love myself and my loving spirit will radiate to others. Abundance of life is emotional well-being along with the achievement of success.

To be successful is to be confident that I can and will succeed at the things that I attempt and to be content with what I achieve. That confidence and contentment cannot be quantified in dollars. I can be successful with a net worth of ten thousand as well as with a million. I am no less successful if my name is known only in my own household as when my name is a household word.

The way to success is most often depicted as a difficult journey. A struggle up a steep, rugged, unpaved, and lonely road. I will struggle to succeed if I set my goals in terms of what others possess or have accomplished. Not everyone can be a millionaire. Everyone cannot be famous. Only one person at a time can be the president. But if my goal is to be happy, to be loved and loving, and to be physically and mentally healthy, I can achieve success with little difficulty. Love, joy, and peace can be had by everyone.

****

Reflect also on: ABUNDANCE, FAILURE, JOY, SUCCEED.

JOY

When what you do and strive to be are in harmony with your soul, joy will fill your life.

There are notable events in my life that filled my heart with joy. Completing high school, graduating from Yale, passing the bar exam, marrying Jacqueline, and witnessing the birth of each of my four children were memorable moments of joy.

And there are on-going events which bring about the same emotion as those special times. My heart is warmed each time a person from the audience tells me that something I said had a positive effect on him or her. When I learn that my life has inspired another to find fullness of life, I am glad. Witnessing the accomplishments of a friend or a family member is joyous. I strive to experience joy not just in special events but in the living of each day.

Upon reflection:

Joy is not simply a transient feeling that comes and goes with a specific event. It is a pervasive emotion that illuminates life. When I am joyful, the feeling is deep in my soul and its presence is evident in my thoughts and can be seen on my face.

Joy is an immediate effect of love. It can be experienced only when I allow love to flow freely. When I act and interact in love, I will experience an inimitable feeling that is bright and warm and sweet. That is joy which makes life's journey a pleasant one.

By contrast, joy cannot be present if hatred and dislike dominate my soul.

It is the law of the eternal universe that joy be the natural emotional state of my being. When it is, I not only can have the abundance of life, but I will experience life's fullness. Though events will occur which will make me sorrowful, my predominant joyful nature will cause healing of my emotional injury. The feeling of joy will soon return.

I can choose whether or not to live in joy. If joy is not my natural emotional state, I can experience momentary feelings of happiness, but those feelings will come and go with specific events. I will be driven by stimuli of physical pleasure or satisfaction in an effort to obtain a fix of happiness.

If I find happiness only in specific events or particular activities, I am destined never to experience the fullness of life. Too much time between the happy activities or events will be wasted in sorrow or sadness.

****

Reflect also on: ABUNDANCE, LOVE, MONEY, SORROW, SUCCESS.

SOUL

Abundant life is experienced only when you put your heart and soul into living.

Granny, my mother's mother, died while this book was in progress. Though she is no longer physically present, my memories of her are quite vivid. So clear, in fact, that some Sunday mornings I awaken and think, "I must remember to call Granny." When she was here, I called her every Sunday morning no matter where I was.

When I remember the things that Granny and I talked about, I feel a continual emotional bond with her. Though she is absent from body, her soul yet lives. Granny and I are still connected in love.

Upon reflection:

The part of me that I know best is that which I can see and touch. That which hungers and must be fed. That which bleeds and feels pain. But that physical body is not me. It is just the casing that I inhabit. I am soul, and therefore, I am eternal. I am an integral and inseparable part of the universe. I am still me apart from my body.

Except that my soul is encased in a mortal body, I am not limited by time or bound by space. I am an intangible being seeking expression in a tangible form.

Every day I satisfy the needs of my mortal nature. I eat to nourish it. I sleep to rejuvenate it. I clean it, clothe it, protect it, and pamper it. I make certain it is exercised and entertained. I spend much time to ensure that others will see just what I want them to see of it.

In my body I am connected to this earth. By my soul I am joined to the universe. Through the latter union I live in abundance.

For my life to be full, my soul must be healthy. A healthy soul is one of love, joy, and peace--love that is not bound by physical barriers, joy that is eternal, and peace that is beyond all human understanding. To keep a healthy soul, I must feed it the thoughts and exercise it with the emotions that promote love, joy, and peace.

When I know the eternal part of me, I become acquainted with possibilities, power, and purpose. I discover how to live the fullness of life.

****

Reflect also on: GOD, LIFE, LOVE, RELIGION, SPIRITUALITY.

MIND

If you keep an open mind, there will always be room for the development of new ideas.

Elois is a blind young lady whom I met while attending activities at the Foundation for the Junior Blind. In a telephone conversation, she tried to convince me to join her religious group. She explained its doctrine and described how her life had been changed and enhanced. Because her beliefs were inconsistent with what I had been taught, I asked questions. When she saw that I would not be easily persuaded, she suggested that I had too much of the "white man's education from Yale" and that I asked too many questions. I suggested to her that she had not asked enough.

Upon reflection:

My mind, like my soul, has no form. It has no color or gender. The shape that it takes depends on what I feed it. Being formless, it can stretch without limit, except the limit that I impose by closing my mind. Curiosity is my mind's yearning to stretch. Questioning is its way of exercising.

My mind is a basic aspect of my being and an integral part of my identity. It is my storage place of data and my processor of ideas, concepts, and opinions. As the bridge between body and soul, it reaches for reality and grasps for truth.

Once I understand something to be real or I judge a matter to be true, it becomes a belief which

I maintain as part of my mental makeup. I am involved in a never-ending process of receiving information and analyzing experiences to assess matters to be consistent or inconsistent with my beliefs.

To have an open mind is to be able to let go of old ideas and accept new ones. The new ideas will come as I receive additional information which alters my judgment of what is real versus imagined or what is true versus assumed.

There is power in what I think and believe. My mental perception of reality and truth governs my physical actions and reactions. My body is my contact with the tangible world and my actions will be consistent with my mental perception of my environment. If I believe that I cannot affect change, I will make no effort to do so. If I believe that there is a god who provides me an unlimited source of power, I will act as though nothing is impossible for me. There is power in positive thinking, but thinking negatively is likewise powerful.

****

Reflect also on: BELIEVE, KNOWLEDGE, SOUL, THOUGHTS.

GOD

Neither the presence nor the power of God can be forced upon you. Through your soul you must invite them into your life.

I was first taught about God in a little church in Compton, California. The family across the street invited my family to attend Trinity Chapel. Only kids went there for the first several years. It was a church founded by a white woman who saw too many black boys and girls playing on Sunday mornings instead of being in church.

I voluntarily attended Sunday school and Sunday worship services beginning at age six years. Church was made fun with the motion songs and the colorful illustrated lessons with cut-out paper characters placed on flannel boards. Through these effective methods of reaching young minds, I was taught that God is my creator and judge. From this I developed a fear of displeasing Him and of being condemned by Him. I was taught that my heart is dirty in the eyes of God and I have to earn His favor by my good behavior. But I cannot be good on my own. I need His help.

Upon reflection:

God is more than Creator and Judge. He is my standard for love and my source of strength. He is my model of perfection and my moments of inspiration. The God that I know is always present with all power to assure that I enjoy the fullness of life for which He created me.

God is a spirit, and that spirit cannot be perceived through my restricted senses of seeing, hearing, tasting, smelling, and touching. If I am to know God, I must believe. But even my mind tends toward finiteness. Hence, through believing I can perceive but a limited aspect of God.

As a spirit, God has no form. The shape that He takes on is molded in my mind. God can be anything to anyone. As a formless spirit, God transcends the limits of time and space. At any time God can be everything to everyone. It is through my soul--that aspect of my being that is both eternal and universal--that I interact with the wholeness of God.

The existence of God is independent of my believing in it. To think and say that God is not would serve only to exclude God from my life and being. The spirit and force of God would remain around me but would not interact with me if I chose to exclude God.

It does not matter how I label that supernatural force that sets the laws of the universe and eternity. For me He is God. To others, Allah. It is a Higher Power or The Force. He can be called Jehovah. God can be male or female. The label is reflective of the finite way that we look at the universe. The label does not determine the nature and character of God.

****

Reflect also on: PRAYER, RELIGION, SPIRITUALITY.

PURPOSE

The sheer joy and certain success of life come from living with purpose, not by chance.

From 1993 to 1994, I served on the strategic planning task force of the government division in which I work as an administrative law judge. After gathering information and eliciting input from those people with whom the division does business, the committee set goals and objectives and wrote a mission statement for the office. It was the latter that caught my attention.

I have heard much talk about setting personal goals. Never have I heard of individuals writing a mission statement for living. I have not written one. Yet I often ask the question, "Why am I here?"

Upon reflection:

There is a reason for my living. The Creative Mind of the universe, in a grand design of abundance, chose the time that my body, mind, and soul should come together. My universal purpose of life is to enhance the lives of others. Given that I have a free will, I choosc whcthcr or not to fulfill that purpose.

Choosing to fulfill my purpose in life, I must discover the means by which I will accomplish it. My individual purpose is the role that I assume in the effort of fulfilling the universal design. My purpose is not dictated by my Creator. Rather, it is determined by my abilities and my desires.

To discover my purpose, I must look first to the abilities and talents with which I have been endowed. The means by which I uniquely enhance life cannot be beyond the functional abilities and special talents given to me by the Creator. If my purpose existed beyond my abilities, life would be frustrating rather than fulfilling.

I next must consider my desires. For life to be fulfilling, it must be joyful and full of love. There can be no joy if my desires are not satisfied.

When I have identified the things that make me happy and feel love in the context of what I am capable of doing, I will have discovered purpose. I also discover that individual mission can be multifaceted, and it can change as my skills and knowledge and relationships change.

Knowing the universal purpose and my individual mission helps me to set my goals. Understanding why I am moving in the direction that I am going makes it simpler to make adjustments in my plans as I confront unforeseen situations. Knowing my mission, I will have reason to hope in the face of despair. Sharing my mission with others will help me to identify those who are with me and those who will work against me.

My life is unique, and its role in fulfilling the universal purpose can be played only by me. If I do not perform my specific role, it will be left undone.

****

Reflect also on: GOALS, HOPE.

2

LIVING THE POSSIBILITIES

In order for it to happen, I first must believe that it can happen, and then I must believe that I have the power to bring it about.

Your position in life is determined not by what happens to you but by your attitude toward what happens to you.

POSSIBILITIES

To think that it is impossible is a self-fulfilling belief which negates the possibility.

The barber, being a Protestant minister, acknowledged the biblical accounts of Jesus' having performed such miracles as turning water to wine and raising men from the dead. But to my inquiry as to whether the barber had performed similar miracles, he responded in the negative. I reminded him that Jesus said, "He that believeth on me, the works that I do shall he do also; and greater works than these shall he do ..." [John 14:12] I would soon learn the reason the minister was cutting hair instead of healing the sick. He did not believe that the words of Jesus were meant for him.

Upon reflection:

Is there anything that is impossible for me to do? Yes, there is. It is impossible for me to perform or undertake anything that I will not accept as a possibility. In order for it to happen, I first must believe that it can happen, and then I must believe that I have the power to bring it about.

If I close my mind to the possibility, it will become impossible for me. My body will only act on what my mind conceives; hence, I am unable to perform the impossible. I must be able to picture it in my mind and believe it to be realizable before I can find the way to bring it into reality.

Within the eternal universe the possibilities

are limited by neither time nor space. Every moment that appears into the present brings with it new possibilities. Things believed to be impossible for humans one hundred years ago are now possible. What I see as impossible today will be reality tomorrow. The possibilities are endless.

If I restrict myself to the tangible, I cannot experience the intangible. If I am bound to the physical, I cannot connect with the spiritual. If I lack imagination and creativity, I cannot tap into the endless possibilities.

Even if my mind is open, beyond my finite mental capacity lies other possibilities. If I do not believe this to be true, there is yet the possibility that I am wrong.

****

Reflect also on: BELIEFS, CAN, FAITH, IMAGINATION, MIND.

DREAM

A dream is a vision of the future, in light of the past, tinted with imagination.

Many times I have been asked by the curious about my dreams. "Are they in color?" "When you dream, do you see?"

I do dream. The ones of recent memory have not been in color. However, I suppose that those that I had before age seventeen were in color since I was able to see colors then. In my dreams, I have always been blind, but I have driven a car, flown an airplane, and chased criminals without assistance. In other words, blindness has not been a restriction on my dream activities.

Upon reflection:

Psychiatrists evaluate sound mental status, in part, by one's orientation to time, place, and person. However, these are antagonists of my dreams. When I dream, the past, present, and future merge to defy the conscious state of time. In a dream I could be living in a house in Saginaw, Michigan, and in no time at all I and the house are in Sedona, Arizona.

And how was it that I, a blind African-American, was elected President of the United States? Oh, it was a dream. Dreams defy the constraints and conformities of the conscious mind.

I do not have to wait until an hour of despair to dream any more than I must wait until night. I can dream during the brightness of the day.

I need only to find myself time and a place when and where neither time nor place matters to me. I can push aside the day's concerns and allow my imagination to roam. I can picture myself walking in the realm of possibilities. In a world where "cannot" is not allowed. I can envision what it is that I want. I can create in my mind the path that leads me directly to what I see.

As I find myself moving back into my conscious surroundings, I should prepare to record my dream. If I do not, it will get lost and forgotten in the limitations of human nature.

My dreams are for nought if they are just remembered. Along with wishing that they come true, I must live to make them reality. I have to put them into action.

****

Reflect also on: IMAGINATION, POSSIBILITIES, QUIETUDE.

EMPOWERMENT

The empowerment of your mind and soul cannot come from another any more than can physical strength be conferred on you.

Arriving home from a day of seventh-grade schooling, I entered my living room to find my great aunt with one of her evangelist friends. I was told that this woman had the power to heal. She could lay hands on my eyes and bring back my sight.

I sat with my head painfully tilted back while the evangelist covered my eyes with her hands and pressed down in fervent prayer. After what seemed to be about an hour, I was released from my torment. It did not bother me that I still could not see. I did not doubt the possibility that my sight could be restored.

Upon reflection:

The possibilities are endless. But unlimited possibilities without the power to effectuate them are pointless. To bring about what I believe is possible, even that which defies my understanding of nature, I must know the source of power.

The power to get what I want does not come from another person. Each of us has the universal right and opportunity to establish a direct line to the source of omnipotence. One who would lead me to believe that my power must come through him does so because he lacks power and seeks to find it by controlling others.

Empowerment and self-empowerment are synonymous. Since power comes from within, no one but me can empower me. I need not wait for someone else to confer on me the power to control my life, to get what I desire, or to realize my dreams. I have already been so empowered. I need only to ignite it.

The mind is empowered by knowledge; the soul, through love. For neither of these do I have to wait for another to give me.

There is indeed power in positive thinking. But the thoughts must be mine and not those of another. I will not ignite power by repeating affirmations unless I adopt them as my own beliefs. My positive thoughts will be the catalyst that ignites my potential.

I am empowered by love. Through it I connect with the omnipotence of God, who is love. In it, I find hope and strength. With it, I can defeat the negative forces that would otherwise deprive me of life. When I let love exist universally and unconditionally, I will sense the power that makes all things possible. I have to share love with others, but most importantly, I must love myself.

****

Reflect also on: ABILITY, CONFORMITY, POSSIBILITIES.

CONTROL

You cannot experience ultimate joy and full satisfaction unless you are in control of your life.

When it came time for me to prepare for life after high school, I sought the services of the California Department of Rehabilitation. My plans were to go to Yale and get my bachelor's degree, get a master's degree from Harvard, and obtain a doctorate from the Massachusetts Institute of Technology. All would be in mathematics. I contacted the Department of Rehabilitation for assistance in obtaining the adaptive equipment and services needed as a blind student. In those days, they were a braille writer, a tape recorder, the supplies used for both, and sighted readers.

The counselor assigned to manage my case tried to dissuade me from going to college. He talked of the successes he had in sending blind clients to a vocational school to learn to be computer programmers. He touted that after only a nine-month course, I could be working and making money. My mind was unchanged. I did not want to be a programmer. A solid college education was more important to me than immediate money.

Upon reflection:

Like putty in my hands, my life in this world can be molded and formed to be what I want it to be. While the putty is yet soft and pliable, I must take control of my life. I decide my educational course, my profession, my vocational pursuits, and my relationships. It is up to me to choose to live in happiness and to seek life's abundance.

Who knows best what I want? Who knows best what I feel? Who knows best what makes me happy? I know best, so I have to take control. If I do not, someone else will. If I do not, the circumstances will. If I permit my parents, my wife, the minister, or my friends to control my life, I will find myself doing things to please others. Doing things to gain acceptance by others. Doing what makes others happy and not the things that give me joy.

Life is given to me to enjoy and to experience success. It is my chance to interact with the people and things of the world. I cannot allow the things that I own or desire to have to control me. I cannot let the pressure from others push me in a direction in which I do not want to go.

****

Reflect also on: CONFIDENCE, DESIRE, EXCUSES, TEMPERANCE, WILL.

DESIRE

Getting what you want requires that you know what you want.

Aside from being blind, I was not much different from my sighted peers. I wanted to play the games that they played and otherwise participate in group activities with them. I climbed trees with other boys and jumped off the roof of my house as did my brothers and sisters. I also wanted to drive when they were learning to drive.

Driving a car was one of those things that most people would rule out as a possibility for me. "How could Dana drive if he cannot see?" they would think. My desire to drive was just the start. I had to find a navigator and someone who would let me use his car. I found both in a friend from church. With his help, I learned to drive.

Upon reflection:

What do I desire? From time to time I must break from my activities to ask and answer that question. I will make time to sit alone in a quiet place to reflect on who I am and what I am currently doing. Am I happy with how things are going for me?

What do I want for myself? It is of utmost importance that I seek to satisfy my desires and not the wishes of someone else. I cannot take a me-only or me-first posture, but my desires cannot be any less important than those of anyone else. I cannot make a total commitment to helping my wife, my children, or anyone else realize their dreams if I do not know how to find mine.

Along with discovering what it is that I want, I must know the wishes of the members of my family. To achieve what is best for the family, I must be sure that the paths to our individual dreams do not run in opposite directions.

What am I doing that I wish no longer to do? I cannot realize my dreams if I am encumbered with burdens that weigh me down. I must get rid of the baggage that I carry that will not be needed when I reach my desired destination. I must free up valuable time that is wasted on activities that do not add to my joy and success.

When I am certain of what it is that I want, I will continually remind myself of the importance of pursuing them. When I am at risk of losing sight of them, I will write them down and read them often. The repetition will serve to increase my appetite for realizing my dreams. A constant reminder will transform my wants into needs. When my desire becomes a need, my will to have my hunger satisfied cannot be weakened by the obstacles that sit in the way.

No more of my precious life will I allow to pass without pursuing the desires of my heart. I will have no one to blame but myself for not getting what I want.

****

Reflect also on: DRIVE, GOALS, PURPOSE, WILL.

GOALS

By setting goals, you determine the direction of your life and give meaning to what you are doing.

I very seldom write them down, but I have always set goals for my life. In my senior year at Marshall High I planned my college education--undergraduate studies at Yale, master's studies at Harvard, and doctoral work at M.I.T. After completing school, I set age thirty as the "deadline" for getting married. When I joined Toastmasters, I made plans for accomplishing the various achievements possible. Setting goals has been so automatic for me that I am amazed when I meet people who function without them.

Upon reflection:

To live my life without goals is like tossing ingredients into a mixing bowl with no idea as to what I am making. I would not know when I had too much of one thing and not enough of another. To function without goals would be like driving an automobile without a destination. I would waste timc and energy getting nowhere.

Indecisiveness, enervation, and stagnation are symptoms experienced by those who are without goals. It is difficult to impossible to make educational, employment, or other major life decisions when I have no direction. I will suffer burnout if I run in a daily "rat race" with no specific goal to achieve. No matter how hard I work, if I am not working toward a goal, I can never get ahead; I cannot know where "ahead" is.

In setting my objectives, I must be specific, realistic, and flexible.

When my goals are specific, my progress can easily be measured. Hence, I will declare what it is that I will do and when it will be done, not what I will be. For example, "I will double my income within the next year", and not "I will be financially independent". The latter is vague; it is difficult to know when I have reached that state of independence.

I must be realistic about my plans or the certain failure will discourage me. It is important to be optimistic and to set marks that will challenge me to do my best. But if I bite off more than I can chew, I will choke. I have to take small steps over short periods of time. The success that I experience will encourage me to step further and faster.

It is important too that my goals be flexible. I need to be able to alter my course when I face an insurmountable obstacle. There is no way for me to know what lies in my path to success, so I must be able to find an alternate route when circumstances so dictate. My plans should always contain an alternative approach to reaching my primary objective.

****

Reflect also on: ACHIEVEMENTS, OPTIONS, PURPOSE.

ATTITUDE

Your position in life is determined not by what happens to you but by your attitude toward what happens to you.

In whatever I attempt, I approach the matter with the belief that I can do it. My can-do attitude is what helped to quell the doubts of the Dean of Admissions at the University of Southern California Law Center. He sent me through a series of interviews culminating in one with him in which he suggested various ways that my blindness would interfere with successfully completing law school. With each question raised, I had a response of how it could be done.

I developed the can-do attitude in response to the he-cannot opinions of many people whom I encountered, prior to meeting the Dean, who doubted my abilities. I sought to prove them wrong. My unwillingness to accept their negative attitudes helped me to find a way to get it done.

Upon reflection:

My attitude is the posture that I take in life. It is my vantage point from which I will view all that happens to me. It is the root of my feelings and thoughts about my surroundings. It prompts my responses to what happens.

I cannot be successful unless I have an attitude of success. I cannot experience the joy of life without a joyful attitude.

A change in circumstances will not change my attitude. I cannot, therefore, wait until things get better to change my outlook on life. I must first change my outlook before I can see that things are getting better.

If my attitude is one of selfishness, I will continue to think of self no matter what the situation. Similarly, if my attitude is one of failure, I will see doom in any set of circumstances. An attitude of optimism, on the other hand, will permit me always to see hope in the midst of chaos.

I can change my attitude by changing what I think and how I feel about a person or event. I must affirmatively establish the parameters of my thoughts and feelings.

I establish love and kindness as the limits of my feelings toward others by affirming: "I will think only of love and kindness, not hatred and ill-will."

I establish the parameters of positiveness by adopting: "I will look for the opportunity in challenges; I will not see them as obstacles."

As I repeat these affirmations, they become embedded in my identity. In other words, they will be integral elements of what I think and how I feel. I will act in accordance with them by habit. The habit becomes the manifestation of my attitude.

****

Reflect also on: FOCUS, OBSTACLES, OPTIMISM.

SUPPORT

The strength and reliability of the support which you can expect from others is based on the way you build relationships.

None of what might be labeled as my major accomplishments could I have attained without support from others. I would not have gone to Yale if it had not been for Harvey's encouragement and help. I would have had a difficult time there and in law school without classmates offering to read for me.

A few months after finishing law school, I received a telephone call from Laura. She wanted to know if I had yet begun to work. When I told her of my efforts and that I had not yet been hired, she instructed me to wait by the telephone. Five minutes after she hung up she called again. Laura had arranged for me to have an interview with Council-woman Pat Russell. Working for the councilwoman was my first job.

Upon reflection:

At some time or another, regardless of my abilities and talents, I will reach the limits of my capacity to act alone and will find that with the help of another person I can go one step further.

I have sought the advise of a friend, shared my troubles with a tolerant and patient ear, ex-changed ideas with a colleague, and joined with someone else in a project or endeavor. When I consider my accomplishments, I see that without the support of others, I could not have done it, could not have done it as well, or could not have done it as easily as I did.

Seldom has a day gone by, or will one go by, that does not involve my interacting with another. Life itself is my opportunity to interact with people. It is interaction with people and not things that brings the joy of life. Since I must interact, I should develop and nurture relationships that are supportive of and not antagonistic to my efforts.

As I pursue my goals, it is more important to build myself a support structure than to form a network. A network is a set of loosely connected relationships. It is useful for obtaining information and catching opportunities. A network is of little use when I am discouraged and need encouragement to boost me up or when I am struggling and must have someone's help.

A network will give way and break if I put too much weight on it; a support structure can uphold me. A net might catch me if I fall; a support structure can keep me from falling. A net is easily unravelled and made useless; a support structure can remain strong even with abuse.

My relationships with family, friends, co-workers, and colleagues are the building blocks for my support structure.

****

Reflect also on: ASSOCIATION, ENCOURAGEMENT, FAMILY, FRIENDSHIP.

3

MAKING IT HAPPEN

I must take my I wants and my I-wishes to a higher level. I will take them to I-did and I-got.

It is not likely that I will do my best and achieve excellence as the result of my efforts if I am not passionate about what I do.

ACTION

You can choose to sit and hope it happens, or you can start to act and make it happen.

My going to college was an automatic step to follow the completion of high school. As far back as I can remember, I had thoughts of pursuing higher education. In my senior year of high school it was time to put substance to the ideas. My plan was to obtain a bachelor's degree from Yale, a master's degree from Harvard, and a doctorate from the Massachusetts Institute of Technology. All would be in mathematics. I was not sure what I would do with the advanced degrees, but I put my plan into action. I applied to and was accepted at Yale, so I could begin the first step of my educational pursuits. I enrolled at Yale on September 14, 1970, my eighteenth birthday.

Upon reflection:

Indeed, success begins with an idea--an idea of what it is that I want to do. It is rooted in a belief--the belief "I can". But my idea is nothing and my belief is powerless if they are not accompanied by action. Thoughts that are not expressed by action are soon fleeting and very soon forever forgotten.

I must act today. I will give my ideas and my thoughts substance. I am determined to put my plans into motion. I must take my I-wants and my I-wishes to a higher level. I will take them to I-did and I-got.

Even if my plans require resources or other components which I do not have, I must act today. I cannot sit around and moan and groan about what I could do "if" or what I will do "when". I must do what I presently can without the resources. I can then take the necessary steps to acquire the additional requisite component. The momentum that will build from my putting my plans into motion will give me a head of steam that will get me over the barriers.

When I begin to put my ideas into action, I invite partnership. My friends and family who see that I mean business about what I intend to do will support and encourage me.

I have been given today's portion of energy, strength, and ability. It is important that I not let them go to waste. They cannot be saved for tomorrow and they cannot be recaptured. I can invest my energy, strength, and ability for their greatest return by doing.

I need not begin my actions by leaps and bounds, though sometimes I will. With patience, one small step at a time will get me to my goal just as well. It is, however, important that I keep on stepping. Each day I must move in the direction of my objectives. If I idle or stall or stop, I will lose the momentum that action gives.

****

Reflect also on: BEGINNINGS, INITIATIVE.

DRIVE

The difference between those who succeed and those who fail is drive.

Passing the bar exam is a requirement to being a lawyer in California. And I decided that I wanted to be a lawyer. I failed my first attempt, getting a score of 1107 when 1200 was necessary to pass. On my second try my score was 1168. The third time was the charm.

In the midst of these attempts, I was laid off from my job and I had to fight the Department of Rehabilitation for assistance with readers to study for and take the examination. My rehabilitation counselor said that taking the bar a third time would not make me anymore job ready. It was drive that got me over these obstacles and to my goal.

Upon reflection:

I can reach my destination of success if I have drive. Drive is the force or the power that gets me to where I am going. There are five essential elements of drive. They are:

Desire: Drive begins with desire. I must know what I want and must set my desire as my goal. The stronger my desire, the more forceful the drive that I will have to pursue my interest.

Resolve: My resolve is manifested in a firm decision to satisfy my desire. I can make my dream come true by choosing the course of life that leads to what I want. My resolve to see it happen will direct me to the plan to make it happen.

Initiative: I must take the initiative to put my plans into action. I cannot wait for someone else to do it for me. The best time to act is now. When I put my plans into motion, I make things happen.

Vision: A clear vision of my destination will help me to avoid the road blocks and barriers that might impede my journey. Vision of the end result gives me something on which to focus, and by focusing on my goal, I am less likely to be distracted.

Endurance: While the force of drive is directly related to the strength of my desire, it can be measured only by my endurance. If I cannot endure to the end, what is the meaning and purpose of drive?

****

Reflect also on: DESIRE, ENDURANCE, INITIATIVE, RESOLVE, VISION.

PRIORITIES

To say you do not have time for it means that you have placed it as a low priority.

Linnea, my younger daughter, who is three years old as I write this, got up this morning asking for hug-hug. To her, a "hug-hug" is to be held and gently rocked. I obliged even though my plan for the morning was to write this segment of the book. For the new year, I set the completion of the book as a priority, and to do that, I decided that writing would be the first thing that I would do each day. But, to deny Linnea her hug-hug was unthinkable. The book would have to wait.

Upon reflection:

As I actively seek joy and success--the abundance of life to which I am entitled--there are great demands on my time. My personal needs, my family, the job, my business, my community, and other pressing responsibilities all cry out for my attention and time. To fit my activities into the time allotted to me, I must set priorities. This is not time management but activity planning.

My first consideration must be my desires. To reach and maintain happiness, I must be doing what I want to do. I must give high priority to the things that I like. Otherwise, life will be a drudgery as I spend my precious, most productive hours on non-fulfilling tasks.

Next I should consider essential activities.

That is, the activity which occupies my time should be essential to achieving my ultimate goal. The activity itself may not give me joy, but it should lead directly to that which does. Those essential activities must be planned and prioritized so that they will be completed in time for me to reach my ultimate objective on schedule.

When I know what I want and what is essential to getting it, I must then consider opportunity. Priority must be given to the things for which limited opportunity exists. For example, I have only one chance to rear my children. If my family is important to me, I must not miss that chance.

Finally, I must prioritize in adherence to deadlines. I have to plan my activities to get the needed things done before their due dates. Many times there are no natural deadlines--that is, deadlines set by someone other than me. I must establish due dates for myself to ensure that I give the appropriate priority to the activity. If the deadline has to be adjusted, that is okay.

Once I have set my priorities, I have a guideline for saying "yes" or "no" to other activities in which I am invited to participate. When I do not have time to do all the things to which I am presently committed, I can drop those things that are lowest on the priority list. If I cannot drop anything because everything has a high priority, I am working too hard to enjoy life.

****

Reflect also on: ORGANIZATION, TIME.

HABIT

If you keep your bad habit of accomplishing nothing, you will become quite skillful at it.

I do not have habits which are typically labeled as bad--habits such as smoking and drinking. However, in 1987, I realized that I had fallen into a routine that robbed me of valuable time for doing what was really important to me. After my daily commute from work, I spent an average of three hours watching television. I would begin with a half hour of local news and another half hour of national coverage. Then came two hours of thirty-minute game shows.

Realizing the amount of time spent in front of the television, I gradually weaned myself from the boob tube. The time that I now spend serving on community boards of directors and writing this book would not have been possible if I were still spending twelve percent of my day watching television.

Upon reflection:

I am a creature of habit. When I consider my daily activities from the time that I rise to the end of the day when I go to bed, I follow routines.

My habits develop because I am a creature of familiarity. I react to the stimuli that are the usual ones. If I do not focus on what I am doing, I will fall into the customary routine even if I want to do something different.

I am a creature of comfort. I will repeat the

actions of yesterday because I know them and am comfortable with them. I form habits and get into ruts because I tend to resist change.

If I do not take care to avoid functioning by rote, I can find myself developing habits that are bad for me. A good habit is one that moves me in the direction of my desired objectives. A bad habit does not. The activity in and of itself may not be bad. What is bad is to spend a significant amount of my time doing something that does not lead me to the joy and fullness of life for which I long.

It is easy for me to develop a habit of doing something that is pleasurable. Such a habit is bad if it consumes time that I could use for lasting satisfaction. An activity that takes an average of one hour a day will consume three full years of my life, assuming life expectancy of seventy-two years.

With willpower and by focusing on my activities and the results they bring, I can break a bad habit immediately. For example, I can end a TV habit by switching it off and substituting another more productive activity in the time slot. I could, on the other hand, continue to watch my favorite program and along with it complete a household chore or write a letter to a friend. Some habits are not easily broken, and I must establish a plan for gradual change.

****

Reflect also on: COMFORT, TIME.

PUNCTUALITY

The person who is punctual places a high value on time, his and that of others.

After finishing law school, my first job was as an aide to Los Angeles City Councilwoman Pat Russell. One of my responsibilities was to attend meetings in the community as a representative of the councilwoman. Initially, I would plan to arrive about fifteen minutes prior to the designated time. However, after the first several meetings, I noted that they would start at least thirty minutes late. Consequently, I started arriving about fifteen minutes after the scheduled time. Thus, I developed the habit of being late to meetings.

Upon reflection:

Punctuality is a laudable personal attribute. When I am prompt, I send the message that I am a good planner and know how to utilize efficiently a limited resource--time--for the maximum benefit. Being on time to my business meeting does not ensure that I will be able to close the deal, but arriving late will significantly diminish my chances of doing so. If I am habitually late or fail to show up at all, I will be labeled as unreliable and will never be able to realize my full potential.

As a person who strives to be prompt, I pursue a goal not desired by all. I can be on time, but I must be tolerant of those who are not. Not everyone has the ability to estimate time as I do.

Some people plan more activities than there is time to perform. Others are in a position to be often distracted by unplanned events. I cannot exclude from my life such late people.

Because I know that activities which involve others may not begin at the designated time, I ought not let that lure me into being a late comer. Instead, I should continue my efforts to be punctual. As I wait for others, I can use the time to prepare for the activity or to relax before the event.

****

Reflect also on: TIME, TRUSTWORTHINESS.

ORGANIZATION

If you want something done right the first time, be organized.

When I began serving as the executive director of the Disabled Resources Center, I had a secretary who appeared to be extremely organized. Within seconds she could place before me a letter that had been written months prior. All I had to do was to ask for it, and if she had it, it would be mine in short order. I found out later, however, that she was not organized at all. She had no system of filing. No alphabetical order. She simply remembered where she put everything. When she left, the new secretary and I had much difficulty in finding what we needed--until we organized the files.

Upon reflection:

I have wasted much time looking for things because I could not remember where I placed them. Often I have had to undo something because I did not do it in the correct order.

To be organized is not a prerequisite for success. Indeed, there are successful people who are not organized. But organization will facilitate my getting what I want or where I want to go.

I can be organized and save a lot of time and effort by following these principles:

Placement--Establish a place for everything that I have. The placement of each is best determined by its usefulness in my daily functioning. If I return items to their proper places, I will have no trouble retrieving them when I need them.

Prospective--My relationships with other people must be kept in the proper prospective. Having such prospective will dictate the nature of and the time I devote to such relationships. Keeping my relationships organized will facilitate my dealings with others.

Planning--My activities must be planned in order to best utilize my time. My plans must include prioritization of my activities.

Preparation--I must be ready to perform the activities of my plans when it is time for each to be undertaken. Nothing exposes disorganization more clearly than the lack of preparation.

Prosecution--I must be willing to carry out a plan of activities with my relationships in perspective and keeping all things in their proper place. Having my things, relationships, and activities organized, I minimize my frustrations and maximize the use of my resources, especially my time.

****

Reflect also on: GOALS, PRIORITIES, SUPPORT, TIME.

EXCELLENCE

Unless excellence is the standard under which you begin a task, it cannot be the result of its completion.

During the several years that I have been employed by the State of California, I have had thirteen assistants to read to me and drive me to work locations. As part of the orientation of a new assistant, I give a lecture about what I expect from her. One significant point of my speech is the importance that she serve as my eyes to give me as much information as possible from my visible environment. However, the more important message is the standard of excellence that I have set for myself. I attempt to impress upon her that I cannot produce excellent work unless she too produces excellent work.

Upon reflection:

I must serve as my own quality assurance manager. I must set for myself a standard of excellence and pursue that standard in all that I do. I have to especially apply the standard when I am giving myself a performance evaluation.

In seeking excellence, I must strive to excel. Not the accomplishments of my colleague or competitor. Not the achievements of my friend or neighbor. I have to strive to excel my own performance. Each day I must make an attempt to do better than I did yesterday. When I use myself as the measuring stick, I can guarantee that sooner or later I will surpass mediocrity.

In maintaining excellence, I must extend myself to new boundaries. Habit and routine will dim my imagination and stifle my creativity. When I get comfortable with performing a task, I will begin to slack off in its high performance. Besides doing a thing better, I must attempt new endeavors.

In demonstrating excellence, I must endure the forces of mediocrity and failure. I cannot lower my standard when others criticize my efforts. I must not allow disappointment to stop me from putting forth my best effort.

In holding to excellence, I must enjoy myself. My best effort is given when I personally identify with what I am doing. My results can be excellent only if I am doing that which makes me happy. If I despair in going to the job, I will not give my best performance.

A natural result of excellent performance is the strengthening of my confidence and enhancement of self-esteem. Confidence and self-esteem in turn enable me to achieve excellence. By contrast, mediocrity will deprive me of the best that is possible for me.

****

Reflect also on: COMFORT, PASSIONATE, PERFECTION.

PASSIONATE

If you cannot passionately embrace it, it will eventually be a burden for you to carry.

When she was just a toddler, my daughter Winter would reach up to me with her arms opened and ask for, "Hug". I would bend over and wrap my arms around her as though giving her a big bear hug. Reacting to my impassioned embrace which had more grunt than grip, she would protest and demand, "Hug-hug." She wanted me to pick her up, hold her, and rock her to sleep. Her demand for "hug-hug" turned out to be the precursor to how she would engage in any activity.
Whether she sits at the television to play a video game, or plays street hockey with the neighborhood children, she puts all of herself into it. She wants it to be perfect and she wants to win.

Upon reflection:
It is not likely that I will do my best and achieve excellence as the result of my efforts if I am not passionate about what I do. My undertaking must engage not only my body but my mind and soul. I can be efficient and effective in the performance of my job by being involved mentally. But excellence in my performance will be achieved only if I am passionate.

To be passionate is to like what I am doing. I will like it only if it is something that I want to do. It must be something from which I can derive pleasure and find fulfillment. I am more apt to experience joy from operating my own business than from being employed by another because of the greater likelihood that I would be doing what I want to do.

The fervor with which I am willing to perform is related to the benefit that I expect to derive from my actions. My need for or desire to have money may induce me to show up on the job, but money alone cannot ignite passion. I will not give myself emotionally to the activity unless my emotional needs are met by what I do. What I do must have meaning and be consistent with my purpose in life.

****

Reflect also on: EXCELLENCE, MOTIVATION, PURPOSE.

PERFECTION

When you have given your all and done your best for a universal benefit, you have achieved perfection.

In my sophomore year at Yale, I had the opportunity to tutor ninth-grade students in Algebra as a volunteer in the Ulysses S. Grant Foundation, a tutoring organization in which Yale students helped high school students with math and English. To keep the attention of the five students on me and the subject matter, I challenged them to prove me wrong. I suggested that they would not be able to; I taunted, "Because I am perfect."

It worked. The students paid attention to every detail to catch my errors. They listened to everything that I said and remembered it. They looked, not only for errors in my math, but also for inconsistencies in my behavior. They found that I am not errorless.

Upon reflection:

So long as I am human, I will err. Yet I strive for perfection. I strive to be complete and to achieve excellence. It is through such efforts that I can obtain the most from life. Those with whom I interact will also be enhanced. As I move toward that goal, I approach perfection. I approach the intent of life itself--to enjoy its fullness.

I was born with many talents and gifts. They were bestowed upon me for a reason. The purpose was not to have something to store away, to hide, or to bury. My talents and gifts are to be used in the pursuit of happiness and success. To be a perfect person--that is a complete person--means to exercise and enjoy all my powers and abilities.

If I am to be perfect, I must use my talents. If I am to reach perfection, I have to discover my hidden gifts and develop them. This is what being a perfect person is all about. It is striving to be what I was meant to be. The process is self-development.

The standard of perfection is to be excellent, not to be errorless. I will always grapple with the questions of what is right and what is wrong and will struggle to maintain my values. I can falter and still reach perfection so long as I do better next time.

Reaching perfection is not easy, nor is it impossible. Its attainment involves an integrated effort of my soul, mind, and body.

****

Reflect also on: ABILITY, ALTRUISM, EXCELLENCE, TALENT.

4

A HIGH STANDARD OF LIVING

If I will not hold to the principles by which I purport to live, they are of little value.

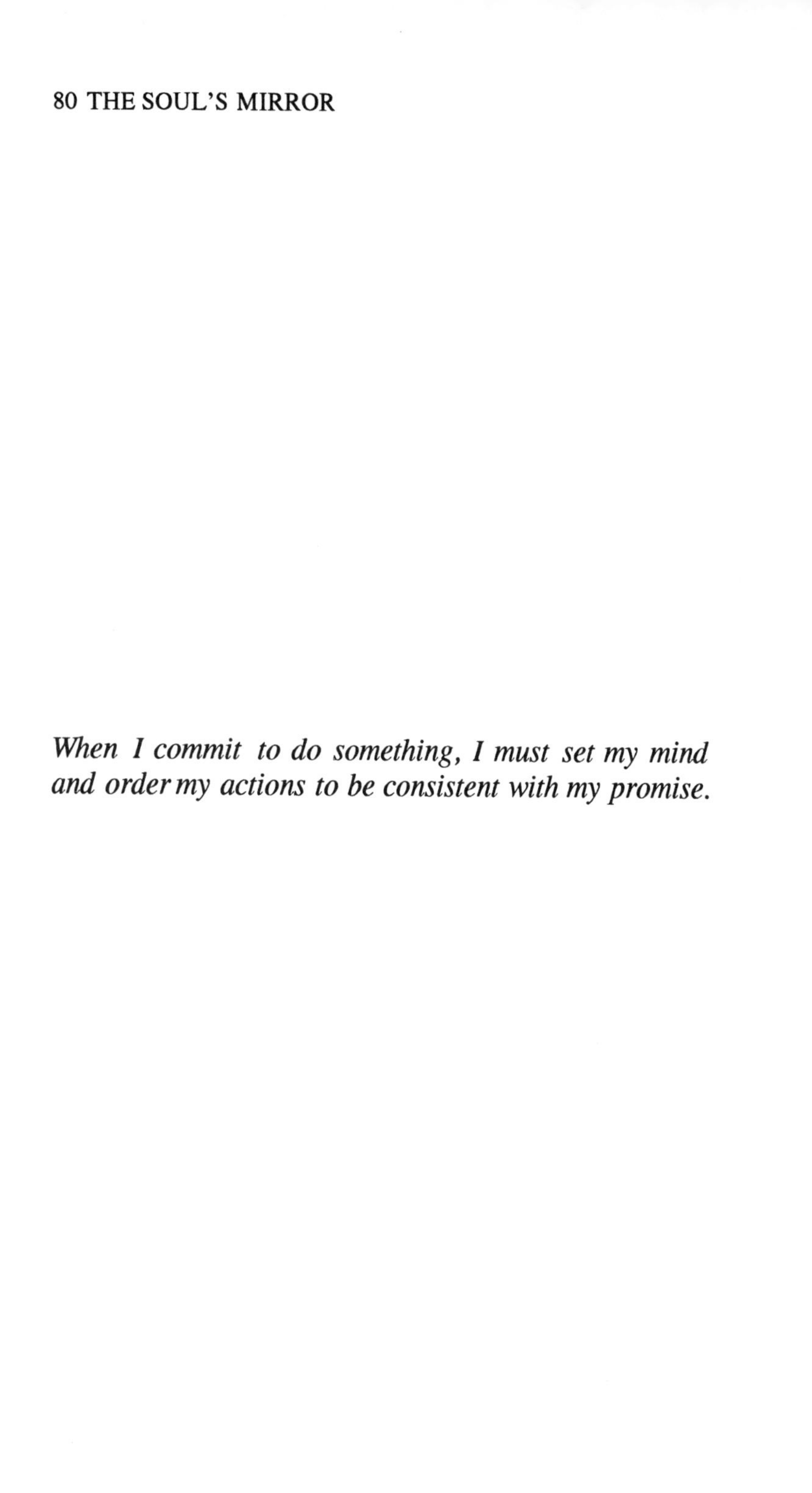

When I commit to do something, I must set my mind and order my actions to be consistent with my promise.

VALUES

The willingness to give up one's values is an indication that you have none.

Twice I ran unsuccessfully for a seat on the Board of Trustees of the Compton Unified School District. Inexperience and naivete were my downfalls in 1983. In 1985, I lost because I would not compromise my values for votes.

Attending one of the candidates forums, I refused to answer a question that would force me to commit to something that I was not certain I could deliver. Each would-be trustee was asked, "If elected, would you vote to fire the superintendent?" It was prescribed that the answer be in the form "yes" or "no" with no explanation. The candidates who garnered the backing of the forum organizers were those who said yes.

Upon reflection:

If I will not hold to the principles by which I purport to live, they are of little value. They are not core values if I demand of others principles to which I do not adhere and which I do not encourage. Core values are those rules of personal conduct that define me, dictate how I will interact with those around me, and delineate what I expect of myself and others. I submit to these three as being fundamental to the success and enjoyment of life: commitment, honesty, and respect.

Without commitment to principles, I have no

values. To have successful personal relationships, especially long-term ones, I must be committed to such. Otherwise, the differences between me and another will cause separation. The optimum benefit in an employment relationship would be obtained if both employee and employer would commit to each other.

How can I function in an environment of misinformation and misrepresentation of the truth? I cannot do so successfully. Hence, I expect of another honesty. I must, likewise, be honest.

While commitment and honesty permit me to join and interact with another, respect allows me to maintain my unique identity. My identity, freedoms, and possessions are protected through respect of person and property. I must give respect to others and what they have before I can expect respect toward me.

Commitment, honesty, and respect are not the only principles by which I function successfully in this world, but the others will find roots in these three. These are core.

****

Reflect also on: COMMITMENT, GENEROSITY, HONESTY, MORALITY, RESPECT, TRUSTWORTHINESS.

MORALITY

The irony of morality is that we are willing to set for others a higher standard than we are able to meet ourselves.

The local high school board of trustees decided to appoint a person, rather than hold a special election, to fill a vacant seat on the board. I submitted my resume in response to the call for applicants. As I stood before the panel, I described my involvement with the schools and my educational background, anticipating that the board was interested in finding a member who could successfully influence the educational program and standards of the high schools in the district. I was then presented with these questions: What is your position on homosexuality? What is your position on abortion?

Ah, there was a member more concerned with my morality. It appeared to me that he was more concerned with having a colleague whose moral views were similar to his than with having a person who was qualified to make decisions regarding education.

Upon reflection:

What is right for me to do? What is wrong for me? My answers to these questions define my morality, the principles by which I will govern my conduct. My moral standard is the set of dos and don'ts and my commitment to abide by them. Commonly referred to as ethics, I also adopt a moral standard by which I will work or operate a business.

My principles of conduct are necessary to control the tendency toward pleasure and survival of my physical being. I set for myself limits on what I will do to get satisfaction and to what extent I will infringe on the rights of others to live.

At the core of my moral standard are my values--values such as commitment, honesty, integrity, fairness, and decency. From my core values emanate a delineation of the acts that are permissible for me.

My moral principles are influenced by culture. What was permitted in my home when I was growing up? What is the industry practice? And they are modified or augmented by education. In school my teacher often told me how to conduct myself in the classroom, in the library, and on the playground. They are governed by societal laws such as the penal code. Finally, and perhaps more recognizably, my moral principles are dictated by my religious doctrine.

My moral standard involves the whole me. I hold the principles of conduct in my mind to govern my physical behavior. But without the soul's involvement, my morality is just a set of rules to be broken. My soul expresses itself by emoting feelings of guilt when I violate my principles.

****

Reflect also on: GUILT, RELIGION, RIGHTEOUSNESS, VALUES.

RIGHTEOUSNESS

Righteousness is finding a harmonious tune and staying on key.

Over the fifteen years that I have been employed as an administrative law judge, I have had several individuals to work as my assistant. All but one have been women. All have had different standards for work performance and for what they believed to be right. I note three of them here. One called herself a "Spirit-filled, born-again Christian". Another was a devout follower of the tenets of Mohammed. The third professed no religion at all. Each falsified her time sheet by recording more hours than she actually worked.

Upon reflection:

I cannot escape the struggle to do the right thing. It does not matter the religion I profess or that I profess any at all. Righteousness is elusive.

The struggle is a spiritual one. From deep within, my soul yearns for expression in harmony with God. I am prompted to love, to honesty, to respect. But my body also longs for expression. It inclines to longevity, craves pleasure, and seeks acceptance. What it will do for survival, satisfaction, or strokes often conflicts with the yearning of the soul.

The battle ground is in my mind. I talk to myself. "I shouldn't." "But I want to." "I mustn't." "But I need to." And then other voices join in.

"You'll be sorry." "Go ahead. Just this once".

The struggle is continuous. Setting for myself a high moral standard intensifies the conflict rather than moves above it. I can give up the fight in order to silence the voices, but a new battle will soon erupt. I may yield to my physical nature thinking no one will know. But I know, and my conscience flashes reminders in the form of guilt.

My physical nature has the upper hand because it is my tangible and visible connection with the world. I see it here; I know it now. Righteousness can result only when I give to my soul that same advantage. I must stay in touch with my inner self. I must be constantly attuned to the harmony of the universe. I must always reflect on my spiritual identity.

****

Reflect also on: MORALITY, RELIGION, SPIRITUALITY.

RESPECT

Seek to be respected for who you are and not for what you have or the position you hold.

Moving to Lancaster, California, Jaci and I looked for a local church for our spiritual nourishment. We visited several. The degree of reception that we encountered varied greatly.

One Sunday we visited a church where we encountered a serious lack of warmth. No member greeted us or welcomed us to the service. On that occasion, we signed the visitors' registry as "Dana and Jacqueline LaMon". On a second visit to that church, we were introduced by the pastor as "Judge Dana LaMon and his wife Jacqueline". After the service, many welcomed us as visitors and invited us to join the congregation. The title of judge commanded their respect.

Upon reflection:

I can give deference to a person because of her position or title or because of his social or economic status, but respect for an individual is given without regard to those factors. To respect a person is to permit individual identity. It is to recognize his or her worth regardless of position, status, ideology, or physical characteristics. Respect is not blind to but rather tolerant of differences between me and another.

To respect an individual is to allow him the same freedom, rights, and privileges to which I believe I am entitled. I cannot simultaneously respect a person and impose my values or ideas upon her. To infringe on the freedom of or abridge the rights of another is to demonstrate a lack of respect for him or her.

Respect is rooted in love. It is an attitude of selfless giving rather than deference with a hope of receiving. I show respect without the person respected earning it. If, however, a person does something that causes me to lose respect of him, he must earn it if he is to have it again.

If respect of others is a valued principle by which I live, it must be universal. It loses its value if I arbitrarily or discriminately withhold it. In other words, respect is shown toward an individual because he or she is an individual and not because of social position or economic status.

****

Reflect also on: ALTRUISM, LOVE, VALUES.

GENEROSITY

The heart and hand that are open to give are also in a position to receive.

My barber and I had a discussion about people in the news who reportedly have billions of dollars in wealth. He complained of a society that included such billionaires while others suffered in homelessness. He declared that if he had billions, he would share it with others. He would go out and help the homeless to find shelter and to get their lives together. I suggested to him that he would never have billions unless by a stroke of luck he came upon it at once. Otherwise, his generous nature would never allow him to accumulate such wealth.

Upon reflection:

Generosity is to the soul as understanding is to the mind. If my mind is opened to new ideas, if my thoughts are allowed to flow freely, if I am ever learning, the result will be understanding. Similarly, generosity is the byproduct of the soul's uninhibited expression of love and its empathetic connection with the feelings of others.

Generosity is not merely the sharing of material possessions. As a characteristic of my innermost being, it will manifest itself in the sharing of feelings and thoughts as well as of my wealth, time, and talents. The mental and spiritual sharing is no less important than the sharing of tangible goods.

The world thrives on the free-flow of benefits occasioned by generosity. The halibut sacrifices life and the orange tree gives up her fruit as food. The sun gives off its rays, clouds let go their rain, and the earth yields her minerals for the benefit of man. Humans hoard. It is generosity, not accumulation, which is the balance of nature.

Altruism is the basis of generosity. That does not mean that the needs of others must always come before mine. To be generous means that I have the ability to subordinate myself to another for the benefit of both of us.

****

Reflect also on: ALTRUISM, GIVING, LOVE.

HONESTY

Though honesty is the best policy, the premiums for it are more than most people are willing to pay.

I felt good about returning to the student store of the high school to let them know of the error that was made. The previous day I had purchased two items for a total of $.45. However, from my $20 tendered, I was given $19.65 as change. I did not discover the error until I got home and counted my change. Explaining the story to the student clerk, who had not been the clerk when the purchase was made, I left a dime on the counter and walked away. She called out, "It would be nice if everyone was so honest."

Upon reflection:

It is not likely that I will ever regain the undefiled honesty that accompanied the innocence of my early youth. There are lies that I told that I cannot call back, items that I stole which cannot be returned, and things that I did which will forever remain my secret. But I can make honesty a cherished principle of living from this moment on.

Honesty is truth. It is not only the faithful representation of the truth but the full disclosure of it. If I am honest, I will behave as though all my actions are in the open and not under cover.

To be honest is to value the property of another. I can be entrusted with anything of value, the owner having the full confidence that it will be in safekeeping.

Honesty requires adherence to established rules of conduct, both personal and professional. There cannot be one without the other. I cannot be a dishonest person in my professional dealings but honest on a personal level. If I am honest, it is a value set in my mind and its display does not depend on the context of my activities. When I deal honestly with another, he or she will have confidence that my dealing will be fair.

My pursuit of success and joy is facilitated if the persons with whom I interact are honest. I must be willing to offer the same courtesy. Everyone would benefit from such reciprocity.

****

Reflect also on: TRUSTWORTHINESS, VALUES.

TRUSTWORTHINESS

A relationship can be no more valuable than the worth of its trust.

During my first summer break of law school, I worked in the office of the Los Angeles City Attorney where I met Annie, a clerk typist. The development of our personal relationship started with lunches and was augmented by daily commutes together since I lived between her and the job. Gaining my trust, Annie began handling my personal finances, including the writing of checks to pay my bills. Eventually, I would have her to write checks to herself to get cash for me. Trust was destroyed when she wrote a check for $75 when I asked for $40. She kept the balance of $35 for herself. I learned of the deception after attempting to cash a check on my own and having the teller to advise that I did not have enough funds in my account. My canceled checks told the story.

Upon reflection:

To have successful and meaningful relationships, I must show myself to be trustworthy. To be worthy of trust, I must convey to the person with whom I interact that he or she can reasonably expect that I am who I purport to be and that I will do what I say I will do. My words may serve as the gauge, but my behavior is the indicator of my trustworthiness.

Someone may place her trust in me and

withdraw it only when I violate the trust. Another will not trust me until he has gotten to know me and found me to be worthy. In either case, I must build on a foundation of honesty and commitment.

To be trustworthy, my words must be true. I should know what I talk about. I must be realistic in my promises. It is better to gain trust by delivering more or earlier than promised rather than to lose it by failing to deliver as promised.

If I am to be trusted, I must commit myself to perform the task, perform it well, and perform it on time. When I am entrusted with another's time, I am given responsibility for his or her life. I must act as though I have been put in charge of something more valuable than money.

****

Reflect also on: COMMITMENT, HONESTY, PUNCTUALITY.

COMMITMENT

The person who is unable to make a commitment is one who cannot be trusted.

To an assembly of friends and family numbering over four hundred, I declared my commitment to Jacqueline Louise Jones. I promised to share with her life, love, joy, family, success, and material possessions for seventy years. (We chose to exclude the morbidity of death from our vows.) That twenty-fifth of June was warm, brightened by the afternoon sun which glowed in a blue sky unmarred by clouds. But the beauty of the day could not match the warmth within me as Jaci and I established marital ties.

Needless to say, after thirteen years, the days have not all been warm, the sun has not always shone, and we have seen some dark clouds in our relationship, but Jaci and I are still committed to living, loving, and pursuing happiness together.

Upon reflection:

If I want to be happy, I must commit to happiness. If I want meaningful relationships, I have to commit to loving others and sharing with them thoughts and emotions. If I want success, I must commit myself to the desires of my heart and the work that it takes to attain them.

A commitment is a promise to myself to keep my word. To dedicate the time and effort necessary to do what I say I will do. I can promise myself to be happy. I can vow to love someone for the rest of my life. It is unconditional. If I attach a "when" condition to my promise to be happy or an "if"clause to my vow to love, I merely declare to make a future commitment to happiness or to love. My commitment would be made when and if a certain set of circumstances arose.

When I commit to do something, I must set my mind and order my actions to be consistent with my promise. The circumstances existing at the moment of my commitment will surely change. Events will occur or options will be presented to me which may contravene the object of my promise. But if I allow my commitment to be the foundation of my decisions and actions, the potential deterrents will not lead me to breach my promise.

My commitment must have a determinable duration--for one year, until the job is completed, for life. Otherwise, it is an empty promise with no value since it may end at any time.

****

Reflect also on: HONESTY, MARRIAGE, TRUSTWORTHINESS, VALUES.

5

WHO AM I

What makes me different from everyone else are what I think and the way I feel.

Others are quick to assess your value from the outside, but your real worth is discovered when you share the treasures of your mind and soul.

SELF-IMAGE

No one can ever see the true image of you until you have a vivid image of yourself.

When people see me, one of the first things they see is blindness. No, it is not that I grope or act helpless, but groping, helplessness, and musical talent are the stereotypical attributes of a blind person. How often do I hear that someone is "amazed" about my accomplishments given my "handicap" or "condition". They are most astonished about my graduating from Yale, attending law school, and passing the bar. These things have been done by men. They have been done by African-Americans. They have been done by African-American men. The amazement, therefore, must stem from the perceived handicapping condition of blindness.

The image that some have of a sightless person must also include something about how he should sound or be able to communicate. In a sociology class at Yale, where students were required to tell of their first impressions of each other, a majority of my classmates said that when I first spoke, their reaction was "Wow, he talks!"

Upon reflection:

The image that I see when I visualize me is that of a person. Not a blind person, not a black person, not a male person, and not an amazing person. I see a person whose essence is love, whose abilities are not limited by physical characteristics, and whose worth cannot be measured by material standards.

To have a vivid image of myself, I must be able to see me from the inside out. My view must be three dimensional.

First, my identity must be complete. My identity cannot be complete until I am in touch with and can freely express my feelings and thoughts.

Second, the assessment of my abilities must be realistic. I must begin my assessment by looking back to the point and time of my birth. At that point and time I knew no restrictions. All things were possible until I began to learn limitations.

Third, the view of my worth must be positive. I am of immeasurable worth. However, my value is diminished by my thinking otherwise, and by my allowing others to judge my worth. I need not and must not let the negativity of others lead me to depreciate my value.

****

Reflect also on: IDENTITY, SELF-ASSESSMENT, WORTH.

UNIQUENESS

Your value is greaterwhen you are one of a kind than when you are one of the crowd.

Jaci and I have four children--four very individualistic offsprings. None is like her or like me though each has characteristics which suggest that they belong to us. The older boy, Dana, is quite reserved and pensive while the younger, Anton, is an extrovert. Linnea, the youngest child, tends to be neat while her older sister, Winter, has to be ordered, pressured, and threatened to pick up her things from the floor. It did not take their parents long to learn that instruction, direction, incentives, and disciplinary actions had to be tailored for each child. We wish them to remain as unique individuals.

Upon reflection:

When I was born, I was destined to be unlike anyone else who had lived or would live in this world. Through my soul, I would feel what no one had felt before. With my mind, I would think what no one had thought before. As a physical being, I was destined to do what no one had done before. It is not that my actions, thoughts, and feelings would be new, but that the series of actions, collection of thoughts, and agglomeration of emotions would be a unique combination. From that combination would evolve desire, imagination, dreams, creativity, and purpose that would be my unique contribution to the universe.

Thankfully, I am unlike anyone else, and it is from differences that life gets its flavor. The abundance of life is experienced only when I appreciate my individualism and love myself for who I am. At the same time, I must recognize and value the differences in others.

I must not allow my uniqueness to be swallowed up by my possessions, my occupation, or my social status. I should not allow the pressure of conformity and the fear of rejection to strip me of individualism. I ought not try to be someone else.

****

Reflect also on: CONFORMITY, SELF-ESTEEM, WORTH.

IDENTITY

When you are known by your thoughts and your feelings, your identity will be unmistakably clear.

The span of my life from age eight to eighteen coincided with the sixties decade. And in that span, I witnessed the evolution of names for my ethnic heritage from Colored to Negro to Black to Afro-American. The last change was taking hold in my senior year of high school.

Vykee, being of the same ethnic group as I, asked me if I preferred being called "Black" or "Afro-American". In our senior year of high school, we were caught up with that social question. I told her that I would much prefer being called Dana. However, if there were a need to refer to my ancestral heritage, she would have to call me an Irish-Franco-Afro-Native-American.

Upon reflection:

Other people around me will identify me by such superficialities as my physical characteristics, my ethnic origin, or my socioeconomic status. They look at my outward appearance and immediately categorize me. But they will never know my true identity until I express my thoughts and show my feelings.

I am a unique individual. Though I may share familial traits with a sibling, or gender features with a friend, or ethnic characteristics with a neighbor, I have my own identity. What makes me different from everyone else are what I think and the way I feel.

If I want people to know me, I have to express my thoughts and share my emotions. They must know me as a man whose feelings are just as important as his thoughts.

When I am certain who I am--that is, when I am in touch with my feelings and can express my opinion, I can then reveal myself to those around me. As often as I concern myself with presenting to others a neat, clean, and attractive outer me, I ought to display the sensitive and reflective inner me. Only when I open up and allow them to look inside will my family, friends, and neighbors know the complete me.

****

Reflect also on: EMOTIONS, SELF-IMAGE, THOUGHTS.

SELF-ASSESSMENT

When you make a realistic assessment of your abilities, you find that limitations are not from within but are in the circumstances.

After graduating from law school, I had a difficult time obtaining a job. I applied to work for several government departments which hired attorneys but all said no. Even the Los Angeles City Attorney for whom I worked during my summer breaks declined to hire me because he did not believe that I could handle the full case load of a new recruit. That was his assessment of my abilities and not mine. Despite the rejections, I maintained unshakable confidence that my blindness did not stop me from working as a lawyer.

Upon reflection:

To move boldly toward the goals that I set, I must make a realistic assessment of my abilities. When I am confident about what I am capable of doing and realistic about my restrictions, the rejections that will inevitably come will have little affect on me. I may be discouraged but I need not be deterred by rejection.

A realistic assessment of my abilities requires two steps. First is the identification of those things that I know from my experience and education that I can do. The list includes innate talents such as speaking, mental skills such as analyzing, and formal training such as my profession. My list can be a mental or written one. It is important that I take the time to develop the list and not be concerned with its length.

The second step of the assessment is to identify my limitations. The limitation might be financial, or it might be functional, such as an inability to see. It might be that I lack the legal requirements to do a thing. An example of a legal restriction is the inability to drive because I do not have a driver's license. In completing this step, always begin with the assumption that it can be done; and never listen to the limitations that others would impose.

For the second list, I must consider things that are within the realm of my desires. For instance, I need not list flying an airplane as a limitation if I do not desire to fly one. If I am optimistic yet realistic, this second list will be short. I will find that I can do most of the things that I really want to do.

****

Reflect also on: ABILITY, SELF-IMAGE, TALENT.

WORTH

Others are quick to assess your value from the outside, but your real worth is discovered when you share the treasures of your mind and soul.

When I was a child, a boy living across the street from me frequently called me "blind bat". An apparent oddity to some on the junior high school campus, occasionally I was the target of small missiles shot from hand-made rubber band launchers. I was called "nigger" on the school campus and again, in a hearing in which I was the judge. The Los Angeles City Attorney would not hire me because I "could not keep up the pace of a new deputy". When they first learned of it, some of my fellow judges complained about my being hired. They said that they needed someone who could help carry the load, not someone whose load they would have to carry.

Despite these negative appellations, acts, and attitudes, I remain convinced that I can make a valuable contribution to those with whom I interact.

Upon reflection:

What is my worth? Is it the difference between the value of my possessions less the total of my debts? No. That is only the monetary value of my accumulations.

Do I measure my worth by the rate per hour or per year that I am paid? No, that too is not a gauge of my worth. It is only the amount someone is willing to pay for my time based on his or her valuation of my skills or talent.

My worth is the value of the contribution I make to my environment, the world, and the universe. I can amass great wealth and still be of little worth. I can be a pauper and contribute greatly to those around me. When I enhance the lives of others while seeking my own success and joy, I add value to those around me and, consequently, to the world. On the other hand, if my living results in the destruction of someone else, I have diminished the value of the world.

My worth is not in my age, gender, race, or physical ability. The fullness of life is experienced not through these physical characteristics but through my mind and soul. My contribution to the life of another is mental and spiritual. Hence, my worth is measured by the thoughts and ideas that I express to others and the feelings that I share. If they are positive, they are of value.

****

Reflect also on: SELF-ESTEEM, SELF-IMAGE, UNIQUENESS.

EGOTISM

The egotist has difficulty seeing the value in others because his view is blocked by the overblown image of himself.

Very shortly after I started giving motivational speeches, I began to feel that I talked too much about myself. I decided that it would be important to include as examples of the principles that I shared the accomplishments of others. I went to the book store and bought a couple of books that discussed the successes of well-known Americans. Before I had the chance to incorporate the experiences of others in my speech, a man shared with me his opinion. Hearing me present to a group of salespersons, he approached me afterward and thanked me for including my personal stories instead of talking about others.

On the other hand, I have been criticized for having too much of me in my speeches. I am still searching for the balance.

Upon reflection:

My life is about me. Living it to the full is about an emphasis on my desires, my abilities, and my potential. But experiencing the sheer joy of life and meeting with its success involves my interaction--physically, mentally, and spiritually--with others. Egotism, therefore, will get in the way of my living in abundance.

Egotism is a distorted view of one's self-image. It is an overblown sense of self-importance. Egotism interferes with my living to the fullest because it causes me to treat another as an inferior. I cannot maximize my enjoyment and success in life by diminishing the importance of someone else.

Egotism can result when I measure my importance by worldly standards--money, fame, degrees, position. Such gauges are artificial and inaccurate. Is the baseball player who receives six hundred thousand dollars a year more important than the high school teacher who is paid forty thousand? Are the contributions of United States President Arthur less important than those of President Carter? That my name may be recognized over another's is no reason for believing that I am more important to the world.

My importance in my surroundings, to humanity, and to the universe is rated by the degree to which I fulfill my purpose in life. This is a spiritual meter of my soul's connection to the people and things in my world. The connection is significant but no more or less than that of another.

****

Reflect also on: SELF-ESTEEM, WORTH.

SELF-ESTEEM

One's assessment of his or her potential to achieve success and experience the joy of life is self-esteem.

One of the most enjoyable classes of my Yale studies was Sociology of Learning. Though there was required reading, much of the class centered on discussions of how and what we learn from interacting with each other. The class met as a whole once a week. In addition, we met once a week in smaller sub-groups without the professor being present. The class of twenty was divided into three sub-groups. In the small groups we shared our educational experiences.

Most unique, however, was that the class selected its own grading system. Our class, which was one of three sessions, chose to self-grade. Surprisingly, not everyone received an "A".

Upon reflection:

Self-esteem is my rating of my potential to succeed, to experience joy, to benefit others, and to live the fullness of life. As the term suggests, self-esteem is my regard for my potential. Because it is potential that is being rated, only I can make the assessment.

What others think of me is not my self-esteem. No matter how well they think they know me, neither my wife, parents, siblings, friends, colleagues, nor any other person can determine my true potential. Their opinions of me are based on their view of life and how they approach various circumstances. I may be held in esteem by others based on what I have done and not on my potential to do.

Self-esteem is not the grading of my past performance. I can fail an attempt and still have a high self-esteem. I can succeed in an endeavor and yet not understand my potential for greater accomplishments.

Self-esteem is not a grading on a curve. It is not developed by comparing my talents, abilities, values, or status to that of another. Such comparison will lead to an attitude of superiority or a feeling of inferiority.

The difference between self-worth and self-esteem is the thing that is being assessed. The latter rates potential while self-worth is the valuation of results.

At each point in time the potential exists for me to live in abundance while at the same time enhancing the life of those with whom I interact. My confidence that I can achieve that point of maximum, mutual benefit is self-esteem. It does not matter whether or not maximum mutual benefit is actually realized. Seldom will I know the full effect of my interaction with others. What is important is that I appreciate my ability and value my role in achieving the fullness and joy of life for all.

****

Reflect also on: EGOTISM, WORTH.

6

DOING WHAT I CAN

When I am faced with a physical or mental limitation, whether permanent or temporary, I can retain or even enhance my ability by increasing my knowledge and/or by strengthening my will.

It is better to get help by swallowing pride than by wallowing in self-pity.

ABILITY

One's ability is not determined by physical and mental capacity alone but by his or her knowledge of what can be done and the willingness to do it.

Occasionally I have the pleasure of talking to elementary school students about blindness, braille, and the special equipment and devices that I use. The students appreciate the opportunity to write their names in braille using the braille writer or with the slate and stylus. They are fascinated with the talking calculator and computer, and they enjoy handling the pieces for the braille versions of games such as Monopoly and Scrabble.

As part of my presentation, I ask the class to list things that a person without sight would be unable to do. Their lists are not unlike the ones I get when I assign the same task to adults. But they are very different from the list that I make for myself. The students' lists are always much longer than mine.

Upon reflection:

I have ability. It is the potential to do what I desire to do. What I can perform physically includes such functions as hearing, speaking, and feeling; sitting, standing, walking, running, and otherwise moving about; reaching, handling, and otherwise manipulating objects. What I can do mentally includes thinking, understanding, analyzing, remembering, and making judgments. My capacity to perform these functions is not, by itself, ability. It is ability when coupled with know-how and will.

Ability comes from knowing what it is that I want to do and knowing how it is done. Once I have gained that knowledge, I must then have the will to do it. When I add knowledge and will to natural physical and mental capacities, I create potential. That potential which waits to be ignited by action is my ability.

Ability is not limited by a restriction in my natural faculties. When I am faced with a physical or mental limitation, whether permanent or temporary, I can retain or even enhance my ability by increasing my knowledge and/or by strengthening my will. With additional information and a strong determination, I can discover the ways to get around physical and mental limitations.

Superior ability cannot come merely from my having a full range of natural capacities. Absent the knowledge of how to use what God has given, I have no potential. Without the will to do, I can do nothing.

****

Reflect also on: CAN, SELF-ASSESSMENT, TALENT, WILL.

TALENT

Talent is like gold. Though it is a thing of value, its worth is realized only after it is discovered.

In the mid- to late-seventies, I had the opportunity to speak to youth in several churches. During one such occasion, I was accompanied by Frank, who introduced me to the usher at the door as the afternoon guest. The usher agreed to take me to my place, and he led me to the piano. It was neither the first nor the last time that the assumption was made that because I am blind, I am musically talented.

The truth is that I have no such talent, unless it is hidden. If so, it is well hidden. My talent is speaking.

Upon reflection:

God has endowed me with the faculties needed to benefit from and experience the fullness of life. When I have a skill that is particularly sharp though I put forth little effort to exercise it, it is talent.

It is important to living in abundance that I learn to recognize and identify the talent that I have. Periodically, I must make an assessment of my abilities. I will not limit my assessment to those areas which we enthusiastically laud and readily label as talent such as singing, dancing, painting, or playing sports. My knack might be in planning, organizing, listening, or teaching. These are also talents.

Though my forte may not earn me fame, it can bring me success.

My hidden talent needs discovery. That is not likely to happen if I am unwilling to try new things.

My recognized talent requires cultivation. To cultivate is to use, to practice, and/or to exercise. It means that I must continue to learn in order to improve in my discipline. Like any other ability that I have, talent has no power if it is not coupled with knowledge and will.

All of my God-given equipment can and should be used to maximize my success and joy of life. However, if I have discovered and am cultivating my special talents, I am certain to find joy in what I am doing.

****

Reflect also on: ABILITY, PERFECTION.

WILL

If necessity is the mother of invention, will is the father.

When I was a youngster in church learning the biblical account of creation, I asked the Sunday school teacher what is it that distinguishes man from the other living creatures. He said it is the free will that God gives us that makes us superior to animals. Yet, I see both inside and outside the church much effort to restrict my free will. Labeling certain actions and conduct as sin which would invoke the wrath of God, I was told what kind of clothes and shoes to wear, how to wear my hair, what kind of music to listen to, who to date, what type of games I could play, how often I should be in church, how much money I should give to the church, and more. The pastor of the church tried very hard to dissuade me from going to Yale, arguing that I should instead attend a Christian college in southern California. The aggregate of the tenets would have taken from me, had I heeded them, the ability to choose for myself and, as a consequence, to live life for me.

Upon reflection:

I am a superior being because I have a will. I have the power to choose the course that my life will take. With such power, I can find purpose in life. I have the power to determine my destiny. With such power, I can move with determination in the direction of my goals.

My will is mine to keep. I cannot give it away

and it cannot be taken from me. I may relinquish control of my life to another, but that is simply an exercise of my weak will. In other words, I have chosen to let someone else determine my course. At any time I am free to exercise again my will and regain control.

I may seek the advice of and encouragement from others, but ultimately it is the exercise of my will that occurs. My will may be weakened or strengthened by the advice or encouragement that I receive.

My ability to do is related to the strength of my will. My capacity to defeat the challenges that I will inevitably face depends on my willpower. When I strengthen my will, I enhance my ability and increase the rate of my success in overcoming obstacles.

The strength of my will is the manifestation of the strength of my desire. How much I need or want a thing determines what I am willing to do to get it. If I develop an appetite to achieve, I will achieve. When I strengthen my desire to take a particular action, I will do it. If I find myself in need, I will experience the power of my will.

****

Reflect also on: CONTROL, DESIRE, DETERMINATION.

CAN

Believe that you can and you will.

I started going to church when I was six years old. Early on I learned a passage from the Bible by the Apostle Paul. The apostle wrote: "I can do all things through Christ which strengtheneth me." [Philippians 4:13.] This passage has meant much to me.

I had to hold onto this reassurance that I too could find strength in God because the people and the circumstances around me would have otherwise pulled me down into the abyss of self-pity and failure. All too frequently I heard others say to me: "You're blind; you can't do it." These words made me bristle in defiance. I wanted very much to prove them wrong. I had to show them that I can.

Upon reflection:

I can. I can. I can. I must affirm these words whenever I hear someone else say that I cannot. Not only must I say them to myself, but I must communicate them verbally and by actions to the inevitable skeptics who believe otherwise.

I must do more than affirm that I can. I must believe it. I must believe that I can enjoy the abundance of life, that I can be a complete person despite my incomplete body, and that I can do whatever it is that I desire to do.

No one can believe for me. It is necessary to have family and friends who will be around to remind me that I can when I am discouraged. Those who would encourage me can only stand in agreement with me. I must be the first to believe that I can.

It is my human nature to avoid failure. Hence, I would never begin a task that I did not believe I could actually perform. If at the outset I am convinced that the result of my actions will be fruitless, I will not make an attempt to do it. Believing that I can do is the spark that initiates my actions.

The thought "I CAN" is not a belief that I am omnipotent and immune to failure. It is the expression of Confidence that my Actions will Net the results that I intend. Such confidence comes from knowledge--knowing who I am, knowing what I want, and knowing how to put the two together. Having such confidence, I will know when I have reached human limitations and must call on the Omnipotent.

****

Reflect also on: BELIEVE, CONFIDENCE, POSSIBILITIES.

HELP

It is better to get help by swallowing pride than by wallowing in self-pity.

At age fifteen, while in junior high school, I started taking mobility training to learn to use a cane. The lessons continued when I graduated to high school. While at Marshall High, my lessons were conducted at and around the intersection of Hollywood and Vine in Hollywood, California.

Initially, Ms. Parra walked alongside me to orientate me to the neighborhood. Eventually, she would give me instructions to follow on my own; she observed from across the street or some distance behind me. Ms. Parra would direct, "Find the tie department of The Broadway; go to the entrance of the Pantages Theater; then meet me at Orange Julius." She would always include a new destination (in this case, the theater) so that I would be forced to ask for help. Asking for help was the hardest thing for me to do.

Upon reflection:

I must not let pride, an inflated ego, or the fear of rejection keep me from asking for help. When I have made a realistic assessment of my abilities and know my true limits, I will find that I can accomplish more by asking for the help of a willing supporter.

Asking for help is not dependence but a way of reaching beyond my limitations. Two friends will form a partnership to help each other in business. A company will hire employees because the demand for the company's product or service cannot be met by its owner alone. Two people will marry to have a lifetime of support in pursuing happiness. Why should I not get the help that I need?

I may need encouragement to move forward to the goal that I set. I may require financial backing for my entrepreneurial endeavor. I may simply need advice on how to tackle a problem. Whatever the help that I need, I must be willing to ask for it.

The worse that can happen when I ask for assistance is that I will be told "no". But those two letters can be the seed for my creativity and innovation. However, lost time, wasted resources, and missed opportunities can come from failing to seek needed assistance.

****

Reflect also on: DEPENDENCE, INDEPENDENCE, SUPPORT.

7

BEING MINDFUL OF LIFE

The success that I achieve and the fullness of life that I experience depend on the set of beliefs under which I operate.

But if what I desire cannot be purchased and appears to be humanly impossible, I must exercise the power of faith.

THOUGHTS

If you accept a penny for your thoughts, you sell yourself cheap.

When Betty was a senior at Yale, I was a junior. I met her in an accounting class and we enjoyed studying together. One day in Yale Station, the university's post office, I heard Betty complain that all her friends were either going to graduate school, getting jobs, and/or getting married. Not so for her. As she pulled the mail from her box, she murmured that all she got were letters of rejection. She was concerned that she was not going to graduate school and did not have a job and was not getting married. I suggested that the reason she was getting nothing but negative news was that she was thinking only negative thoughts. I encouraged her to change her thinking.

A week later, meeting again in Yale Station, Betty joyously announced to me that she got a job. She told me that she had followed my advice and started thinking positively about her future. Two years after her graduation, I received from her an invitation to her wedding.

Upon reflection:

I am a unique individual because of what I think. My thoughts and my feelings are inextricably intertwined. What I think affects how I feel, and how I feel influences what I think. They both are responsible for what I do. In other words, my mind and soul control the actions of my body.

I will think love. I will think of peace. I will think on the things that bring me joy. I will let these thoughts dwell in my mind, and they will keep out hatred, conflict, and sorrow. It is necessary for me to take affirmative steps to keep positive thoughts in mind.

I must think power. I must think of possibilities. I must think on all of the things that lead me in a positive direction. I must concentrate on these thoughts. I must allow them to be a part of me. I will then feel the love and peace and joy and hope that come with these thoughts.

My mind is continuously at work processing information that I input. New thoughts are created and old thoughts are recalled. Unwittingly, a thought will flash, leaving as quickly as it came. I cannot always keep unpleasant thoughts from crossing my mind, but I need not let them settle. I will not dwell on the negative.

What I read, what I hear, and what I watch are sources of food for my thoughts. A constant diet of negativism--violence, personal conflict, human despair--in my entertainment will cause my life to develop the same characteristics. If I put garbage in, I will get garbage out. I must choose a diet for my mind that will build healthy, creative, and powerful thoughts.

****

Reflect also on: BELIEFS, EMOTIONS, IDENTITY, MIND.

BELIEFS

The realm of possibilities within which you will operate is defined by what you believe you can do.

In my junior year at Yale, I was asked by the admissions office to give Adrian, a blind applicant, a tour of Yale's campus. It was hoped that the evidence of my getting around with a cane would be proof enough for him that it could be done. Adrian telephoned me a couple of weeks after our tour to say that he would go to Amherst because the Yale campus was too large. I remembered thinking the same about the University of California at Los Angeles even though Jerry, a blind student there, found it maneuverable.

Upon reflection:

The success that I achieve and the fullness of life that I experience depend on the set of beliefs under which I operate. I cannot attain success if I do not believe that it is possible for me.

What I believe has evolved from my experiences and from what I have been taught. Though I may not always be able to articulate them, I have adopted a set of beliefs that defines my perception of the world, directs my attitude toward life, and determines the nature of my relationships with others.

If I perceive the world to be finite, then for me the possibilities of what can be achieved will be limited. I can attain the limitless possibilities of greatness only when I believe that I have the capacity to tap into the endless resources of the universe.

If I believe that my life is subject to chance, I will make little effort to take control of my destiny. If I assume the worse, I will see the worse even if better sits right next to it.

I cannot develop and strengthen meaningful relationships with others if my beliefs about people grow out of cynicism and distrust.

I have adopted the following set of beliefs to be the foundation of complete success and ultimate joy:

> I am an integral part of the eternal universe and have the ability to tap into the omnipotence of God.
>
> I am entitled to abundant life.
>
> Every event of my life can lead to my joy and success.
>
> All things which enhance life are possible.
>
> My life is enhanced when I contribute to the joy and success of another.

If I close my mind to any one of these, I eliminate the possibilities it can bring.

****

Reflect also on: BELIEVE, CAN, KNOWLEDGE, MIND, POSSIBILITIES.

KNOWLEDGE

The size of your world is directly proportional to the range of your knowledge.

I sat in Mrs. Lamoureau's class marveling at the ability of the other nine students to answer the questions that the teacher posed. I was in the fourth grade. It was my first year at Frances Blend, a school for the blind located in Hollywood. I was bussed from Compton, where I had previously attended school. It was immediately apparent to me that my classmates knew more than I knew. Each time the teacher asked a student a question about geography or history or science, the student was able to answer. But I did not know the answer. I hoped with all my being that she would not call on me. I did not want to be embarrassed by not knowing and by giving the wrong response. To avoid that potential humiliation, I set out to learn as much as I could.

Upon reflection:

The instant that I was born I began accumulating knowledge. Like a sponge my mind began sopping up facts, figures, and concepts. It was not through formal instruction but through experience.

My innate desire for knowledge stems from a mental tendency toward truth and reality. Just as the body cannot move both forward and backward simultaneously, my mind will not retain information or beliefs that lead in opposite directions. As new information is gained, I automatically send it through a test of consistency. I reject it as being inconsistent with my concept of truth and reality or I accept the new and reject the old as no longer useful. Understandably, I am more apt to accept as truth my first knowledge on a particular topic because it is likely not to be inconsistent with information which I already possess. However, if I know something about the topic, it is difficult for me to accept new but conflicting facts.

The knowledge that I gain is the raw material for my thoughts, ideas, and beliefs. If I feed the mind information of little value, I will produce worthless thoughts and ideas. If I limit my knowledge intake, I will limit my creativity and innovation.

I should seek to know as much as I can. The more that I know, the closer I move toward omniscience. The more I become like God, in whose image I was fashioned. The greater the power I can exercise over my circumstances. There is power in knowledge.

****

Reflect also on: EXPERIENCES, LEARNING, MIND.

EXPERIENCES

We can gain knowledge of the tangible through teaching, but the intangible is learned only through experience.

Greg and I would stay up late while he talked about Kathy. It was the summer of 1973 and the three of us worked in a tutoring program on the Yale campus. Kathy was his first love, and Greg demonstrated the usual excitement that comes with the hope of a new romance. I wanted to temper his emotions; I wanted to save him from pain. I knew that Kathy did not share the same romantic feelings toward Greg as he had for her, but I could not tell him what Kathy told me. When it comes to matters of the heart, learning is best gained through experience.

Upon reflection:

Even before I was taught facts and figures, I began to understand feelings and personal interactions through experiences. In the very first hour of my life, I started storing information and formulating beliefs about myself, about other people, and about life. That experiential learning is a continuous educating process.

I can learn about my tangible environment and things external to me through physical interaction or by communicating with someone else who knows. But I can only learn of and understand what is inside me--my feelings and thoughts--through experience. A friend can tell me about love, but I understand it only when I experience it. I can read about the power of positive thinking, but until I act upon what I have read, my knowledge is incomplete.

I ought to cherish, rather than curse, the things that happen to me, even if they cause me pain. From that pain I can learn. I develop an understanding of my emotions and develop skills to interact with the universe beneficially.

I have to maintain the attitude that there is a lesson to be learned from what I go through. If my analysis of the situation reveals no lesson, I can share my experience with a friend. His or her objective prospective may shed light that will be revealing.

Because I realize that my experiences, negative as well as positive, are for my education and edification, I will not permit myself to be governed by circumstances. I maintain control of my life by extracting from events their lessons and moving on.

****

Reflect also on: ADVERSITY, KNOWLEDGE, LEARNING, OPPORTUNITY.

BELIEVE

Through believing you can see and touch your future.

I became blind when I was four years old. But sight is all that I have lost. I still am able to hear, to smell, to taste, and to feel. I can appreciate the early-morning chirping of the birds. When my wife bakes a chocolate cake, I know it. When I step out into a frigid winter day, I can feel it. But the beauty of a blue sky line pierced by snow-capped mountains, I must accept as true from the description of another. I must believe. Believing allows me to fully appreciate my surroundings.

Upon reflection:

I now have available to me only four innate faculties for exploring my surroundings--hearing, touching, smelling, and tasting. These four senses are physical and by their very operation are restrictive. They limit me to what I can personally experience. They allow me to interact with my immediate surroundings only.

My most powerful tool for exploring the world is a mental one. It is believing. By using this faculty, I transcend the limitations of person, place, and time. Though I experience a restriction in sensory perception, I can yet appreciate the things that are viewed by those who see because I believe.

The world that I know goes beyond the range of my physical perception. Because of what someone else has experienced or felt of which I have read or been told, my knowledge of the world extends far back in time; it goes around to the other side of the globe; it reaches beyond the earth. All because I believe--that is, I accept as being true what has been communicated to me.

More important, I can know things that are beyond the realm of human experience. I know God through believing. I have not heard with my ears a sound that is God. I have not felt with my hands an object that is God. Because I believe in the existence of God, however, I have felt the Spirit and have experienced the Omnipotence of God.

Since believing is not subject to time or space, I can use it to explore and shape the future. Where I will be and what I will be doing next month, or next year, or five years from now is impacted by what I believe.

****

Reflect also on: EXPERIENCES, FAITH.

IMAGINATION

Imagination that is allowed to roam will find the way to reach the desires of your heart.

In my motivational presentation "The Driving Force", I ask the audience to imagine a blind man driving. Nine times out of ten the audience laughs. That response is an indication of the difficulty to imagine such a situation. On the other hand, I receive immediate responses from several individuals when I ask them to imagine life tomorrow if today they were to receive ten million dollars. Why the different reactions?

I had no difficulty imagining myself operating a motor vehicle. With an understanding of my limitation and what was needed to drive, I could imagine how to bring the two together.

Upon reflection:

Imagination is a powerful mental tool available to me. It is the catalyst for creativity and the definition of dreams. Through it I can search the extremities of the universe. To keep it sharp I must use it regularly.

To allow my imagination to roam, I must shed the limitations of my present situation. I must forget about my physical being--my age, race, gender, strengths, and weaknesses. I must ignore my social conformities--where I live, where I work, what I possess, and how much education I have. Then I can ignite imagination by asking the question "what if."

My what-ifs must be positive.

I have to avoid the snares of negativity as my imagination roams. When I respond to the what-ifs, I must bypass all the nots. "It cannot happen", "I have not seen it happen", and "I have not seen one before" are unacceptable responses to what if. The universe is of unlimited possibilities. I can keep searching until I find what I need in order to bring a clear picture into focus. When I create the ideal situation in my mind, it will aid me in finding that situation in reality.

As I let my imagination move past my present limitations, I will find that my mental picture will begin to reflect the deep desires of my heart. If I exercise my imagination repeatedly, the picture will become clearer and more focused.

****

Reflect also on: DREAM, FAITH, POSSIBILITIES, QUIETUDE.

FAITH

Faith is unquestioned belief that it can happen coupled with the expectation that it will happen in the absence of any evidence that it should happen.

From September 1975 to October 1978, while teaching Sunday school at a small church in Compton, California, I developed a heightened interest in the power of faith. My curiosity was spurred by the biblical passage at Matthew 17:20, "If ye have faith as a grain of mustard seed, ...nothing shall be impossible unto you."

I acquainted myself with "faith ministries" but was disappointed with their teachings. The emphasis on the material wealth that faith could garner seemed to be a mockery of Jesus's assertion. I had seen plenty of evidence that tangible possessions could be had without faith.

Upon reflection:

If what I seek is money, I can devise a scheme for getting it. I do not need faith. If what I am looking for is recognition and praise, I can learn what is being rewarded and do it. I do not need faith. But if what I desire cannot be purchased and appears to be humanly impossible, I must exercise the power of faith.

The object of faith is born through imagination. Faith requires that I open my mind and set my imagination free from the bonds of human nature. When my imagination is joined with desire, I can conceive what man is powerless to perform but faith can bring it to fruition. Faith permits me to exceed the limitations of what I see, hear, and touch in the physical world.

What my imagination conceives must be nurtured in hope. Hope will lead me to the expectation that it can occur. Because there will be no tangible evidence that what I imagined can be realized, I will have doubt. My questions of its possibility will diminish with the swell of expectation, and all my questions must be resolved before faith can work.

Faith is more than positive affirmations. My verbal reminders of the possibilities are necessary mental preparation, but I must do more than say it. I must believe that it is possible. When my belief becomes strong and firmly set in my mind, I will begin to act in conformity with my faith.

****

Reflect also on: BELIEVE, DOUBT, HOPE, IMAGINATION.

8

THE FEEL OF LIFE

When I allow it to do so, love infiltrates my mind. It encompasses my thoughts and feelings.

Though I may not be able to control those external conditions, I can find in them, or despite them, a reason to hope.

EMOTIONS

A clear reflection of your soul comes to light when you are able and willing to show what you feel.

It was a Thursday evening and I needed to prepare for a preliminary hearing in my first case. I was due in court the next morning at 9:00. My client was charged with armed robbery. I needed to get to the law library to do some research. I could find no one to assist me. The more I searched, the more angry I became with being blind and having to depend on another for assistance. When the evening waxed too late to go to the library, I lay on my bed and cried out my frustrations. A man shedding tears? An attorney showing emotion?

Upon reflection:

Anger, pleasure, love, hatred, joy, sorrow, despair, hope, fear, and courage are only some of the emotions that a healthy soul is capable of feeling. They are natural and they are good.

As natural and involuntary as my heart beats, I feel. What I feel is influenced by what I think and is reflected in what I do. I am affected emotionally by what I see, hear, or otherwise perceive. I react emotionally to the circumstances around me.

My feelings emanate from my soul as my thoughts, from my mind. I am who I am because of how I feel as well as what I think. I am balanced when I can act with both feeling and reason. If I act without feeling, I will be as much out of control as when I act without reason. The key to my balance is control.

I strive to let love be the basis of all that I feel as I endeavor to have thought accompany every action. Then I will be in control. When I get angry, for example, I will do so in love and carefully weigh the consequences of my response to my anger. To find pleasure or joy which is based in love is to delight myself in that which promotes positive thoughts, feelings, and results.

I have before and will feel again emotions such as despair, sorrow, fear, or anger prompted by events which occur in my life. These emotions need not permanently dwell within. They do not have to be characteristic of my identity. If I love--love myself and love others--I can replace the negative emotions with hope, joy, courage, and contentment. These emotions flow naturally from love.

****

Reflect also on: BALANCE, IDENTITY, LOVE, SOUL, THOUGHTS.

LOVE

Even if you suppose that love is blind, you must remember that it can still feel.

It is not unusual for my youngest child Linnea to plant on my lips a soft kiss accompanied by "I love you, Daddy". She does this with her brothers and sister and with her mom. I was surprised, however, the other day when, as we two sat at the dining table, she stood up in her chair, pushed her face next to mine, and said, "You love me, Daddy." It was not a question but clearly a statement of fact. How my three-year-old understood it is remarkable. I do not often express it in words.

Upon reflection:

Love is the very essence of my being. It emanates from my soul and connects me with the eternal universe. When I allow it to do so, love infiltrates my mind. It encompasses my thoughts and feelings. It being the foundation of thoughts and emotions, I can find my identity in love. Love then is manifested in my physical being. It is through my look, my touch, my speech, and my actions that love finds expression.

Because it is the essence of me, love need not be taught. It is understood and felt by a newborn. It is experienced and expressed by a young child. Only as we mature to adulthood do we lose the capacity to feel and express love without reserve. My reluctance to let love exist in its free-flowing state results from my confusion of love with physical desire. From association of love with unfortunate experiences. From misidentifying love with pain.

Love lives forever and is, therefore, life. I can ignore it, suppress it, hide it, abuse it, misuse it, attempt to destroy it, think without it, act without it, but I cannot kill it. Its inclination is to flow unbounded and unending. I, however, must permit it to do so.

It is through love that I connect and interact with the universe and with my immediate surroundings. Without love I am only another physical mass in the world. Through love I am one with it. I can only truly know another when introduced by love. Love permits me to understand the thoughts and emotions of another. Even the real beauty of nature and the things she produces can be fully appreciated and enjoyed only in love.

****

Reflect also on: HATRED, JOY, LOVING, SOUL.

SORROW

It is through expression not suppression that the soul finds fast relief from sorrow.

I put my arm around Penny's shoulders and held her close. I wanted her to feel the warmth and the strength of my love for her as she expressed deep sorrow over the loss of her mother. I had no intentions of stopping the flow of her tears. Sitting in the funeral service of her mother, it was natural for Penny to cry. It was understandable that her sorrow would be great, her father having died only two years prior. Both parents died before they reached their fiftieth birthdays.

Penny, a young lady of twenty-one years, called me from New Haven, Connecticut, and asked that I attend her mother's funeral. She wanted someone to comfort her. She told me of her father's death and how she had not cried because her brothers and sister expected her to be strong for her mother. Now her mother was gone. I was on the plane the next day from Los Angeles.

Upon reflection:

Sorrow is the emotional pain that comes when I lose the object of or a source of love. When love is repressed, when it is unrequited, when it cannot find an outlet, I feel sorrow. This is so because my soul's natural tendency is to love.

I will permit myself to grieve over the loss of a loved one. Like physical pain, the sorrow that I feel is a beneficial warning sign--a sign that all is not well emotionally. I will shed my tears freely; by doing so, I begin the healing process. Along with grieving, however, I must open myself up to love and to be loved.

Sorrow cannot be relieved by words alone. Even the words I read right now will not console me at the time that consolation is most needed. Words are for the mind. In times of sorrow, it is my soul that is most in need. These words serve to prepare me for the time when sorrow comes.

Healing will come when I find another outlet for the love that I long to give or when I accept another source for the love that I need. Healing will come quickly when I have a strong support system--when I am encircled by many with whom I share love. By sharing love, I not only assure myself of a source of consolation, but I can be a solace for someone else who is in sorrow.

****

Reflect also on: JOY, LOVE.

HOPE

As long as there is life, there is hope.

When my wife Jacqueline was pregnant with the first of our four children, she had a problem which required that she be hospitalized. The doctor who conducted the initial examination concluded that our baby could not be saved because too much embryonic fluid had been lost. A second doctor, who examined Jaci a couple of hours later, concluded the same. Later on in the day, after Jacqueline had been sent to the labor room with drugs to induce contractions, a third doctor took an ultrasound and found that the baby was alive with plenty of fluid. That doctor found for despairing parents reason to hope. He prescribed bed rest and the pregnancy was a successful one.

Upon reflection:

Hope is not a tangible object that one can give to or take from me. Hope is found within me. The external factors such as a doctor's prognosis, the state of the economy, or the circumstances in which I find myself are simply the bases for hope. Though I may not be able to control those external conditions, I can find in them, or despite them, a reason to hope.

To hope is to *H*ave an *O*utlook for *P*ositive *E*xpectation. There is no meaning to hope and no reason to consider hope if there is nothing that I expect to occur. My expectation must be positive.

To expect something negative to happen to me is to despair.

There is light at the end of the tunnel. It is my choice to see it as the hope of the end of my dark surroundings. Even if I despair that the light is of an oncoming train, hope can still be found. I can see it as my chance to hop aboard and ride rather than to allow it to run me down. When I look for the positive result--the result that is to my benefit, I can find a reason to hope.

****

Reflect also on: DESPAIR, FAITH, MOTIVATION.

GUILT

Living with excessive guilt is as harmful to your soul as living with no guilt at all.

I knew instantly that I had done something wrong when I ripped in half the Mother's Day card that I had made for my mother. It was a third-grade school project. I liked it and could not wait for Sunday to present it to my mother. But my brothers and sisters kept teasing me about it. They made me so angry that I tore the card up and threw it in the trash. And then I felt bad. Guilty enough to want to undo my action. The best that I could do to remedy the problem was to present the pieces to my mother. She showed appreciation as though the card were whole.

Upon reflection:

There is nothing wrong with guilt. Like fear or anger, it is a feeling which, properly placed and in balance, prompts me to action or prohibits me from acting so that I can enjoy the fullness of life. It is misplaced or excessive guilt that interferes with living.

For what do I feel guilty? Is it for a wrong that I committed or an act of omission that was rightfully my responsibility? If so, I must deal with and release myself from the guilt. I must accept the blame, seek forgiveness, and be satisfied that I paid the price for my action. Denial, running, and hiding will not permit my soul to let go of the guilty feeling.

In accepting blame, I have to accept only that which is rightfully my responsibility. I alone must determine what is rightfully mine. I should not let others push their blame onto me. They do it in an attempt to release themselves from guilt. I must not carry the guilty burden of my wife, family, friend, or other person. I ought not hold on to guilt for events over which I had no control.

When I have admitted wrong and sought to be forgiven from the persons I injured, I must forget it even if they do not. While I may yet have to pay for the consequences of my wrong, there is no reason that I must suffer with guilt.

Excessive or misplaced guilt--like excessive or misplaced anger, fear, sorrow, or other feelings--is a sign that my emotional health is in jeopardy.

****

Reflect also on: MORALITY, RELIGION.

COURAGE

It takes courage to stand for what you believe when you know that even your friends may leave you standing alone.

In the late seventies, I was very active in my church. I attended almost every service. I taught the young adults Sunday school class and was administrative assistant to the pastor, sharing with him the task of delivering the Sunday morning sermons. At the pinnacle of my involvement the pastor presented me with the choice of resigning from my positions of leadership or terminating a friendship that he thought inappropriate for me to maintain.

The problem that the pastor saw was that the young lady whom I befriended was under eighteen years old. I saw no problem with discussing the Bible and school education with her. That was the extent of our relationship at the time the options were presented. I saw no conflict between my spiritual principles and the relationship, and I did not think that someone else should choose my friends. So I resigned.

Upon reflection:

It is natural for me to desire the approval and acceptance of my colleagues and contemporaries. It takes courage, therefore, to make a decision that is unpopular. It also takes courage to say "no" to a sought-after opportunity when to accept it would compromise my values.

Courage is not physical or mental. It is a fire that emanates from my soul. It is the impetus that moves me forward fearlessly in the face of difficulties and confidently on the path that I have chosen. When it is summoned, its effects will be felt both in my body and in my mind as well as in my soul.

If I have not chosen a course for my life, I need no courage. It does not take courage to drift with the wind or to jump on the bandwagon. It takes courage to choose a course for my life and to stay on that course despite obstacles and opposition.

If I have no fundamental principles on which I stand, I need no courage. It does not take courage to make the decisions that please the crowd. Courage must be summoned when I need to make that decision that is true to my values but will not get me the nod from others.

When I am confident that I have chosen the right course but uncertain of what lies in my path, with courage I can take the next step and keep moving toward my goal.

****

Reflect also on: CONFIDENCE, GOALS, VALUES.

LONELINESS

Loneliness is not the result of physical isolation but of the soul's deprivation of requited love.

I was admitted into General Hospital on December 4, 1961, for my third eye surgery. My mother was with me during admission. However, she herself was admitted later that day for the birth of my youngest brother. So she did not visit me at all. The sixteen days that I stayed in the hospital were lonely ones. I was in a semi-private room, but the other half of the semi was never admitted. Santa Claus visited and brought me toys. I had fun playing with them during the day. I went down the hall to the men's ward to talk. But at night, I peered out the window, longing to be freed from my prison. Longing to be in touch with the people I loved.

Upon reflection:

I am not alone. Millions after millions have experienced the same feelings of isolation. Of loneliness. That feeling is the longing of the soul to be in touch. It is the pang of love yearning for sustenance and cxpression. The feeling may come when I am physically alone, but it can arise when I am in the company of others.

I ought to take the initiative to satisfy that longing to be in touch. I can call a friend to let her know that I am thinking of her. Who knows? At that moment when my call is made, my friend may also be feeling lonely. My contact will help both of us to cross the gulf of isolation.

My hour of loneliness can be moments of inspiration and creativity. I can express the love that pushes at the seams to flow out in the words of a letter. A poem. A song. Even if my written words are never shared with another, I will feel good about having expressed my emotions.

I am not alone. The Supreme Being of the universe is in reach. If I reach out with my soul, I can touch and talk with the ultimate source of love. I can spend the moments of quiet isolation to listen to my heart as Love speaks.

****

Reflect also on: FRIENDSHIP, PRAYER, QUIETUDE.

DESPAIR

When failure causes you to despair, it is a sign of your commitment to succeed and not an indication that you should quit.

I could not wait to receive a letter from the Committee of Bar Examiners to find out if I passed the exam on my second try. I telephoned on the day the results would be published and learned that my name was not on the list of those who passed. I despaired.

Although I considered my first failure as a learning experience, the second caused me to question my abilities and my decision to enter the legal profession. I cried a little and then directed my attention and energy from failure by working on a complex macrame project. Successfully completing the plant hanger, my desire and confidence to pass the bar were rekindled.

Upon reflection:

I am not immune to disappointment or failure, so from time to time I will experience despair. My feelings of hopelessness should be temporary and should not bar me from reaching my goals.

I will consider the following when I despair:

1. Do not hold back my tears. This physical release will help to heal the emotional injury. It is natural to cry even though I am a man.

2. Do not make decisions concerning the pursuit of my goals. The hopeless feeling will cause me to question my abilities and the wisdom of my efforts. That is not the frame of mind within which to make my important decisions. If I decide to quit, I should do so when I am in a state when reason and emotion are in balance not when I am overtaken by emotion.

3. Divert my attention from the disappointment or failure. I should find a source of entertainment. I can take a trip to change my surroundings. I should undertake a project that emphasizes my strengths and gives me joy. These are ways to restore emotional well-being.

4. Share my hurt only with someone who is certain to empathize with and encourage me. In my moments of despair I do not need anyone else to rub salt in my wound--the "I told you so" person.

****

Reflect also on: ENDURANCE, HOPE, QUITTING.

FEAR

Since the object of fear is often imaginary, to conquer it is to open your mind to consider other possibilities.

I have never liked going to the dentist. I understand the need for clean and strong teeth and healthy gums, but I am afraid of injections. Specifically, I fear the pain that an injection can cause. Ironically, if I would not allow my fear to keep me from making regular visits to the dentist, I would not require the treatment that necessitates an injection.

The truth of the matter is that I have never experienced pain from a needle any worse than from hitting my thumb with a hammer. But pain from the latter has never stopped me from nailing.

Upon reflection:

Fear is a feeling which can significantly diminish my potential for enjoying the fullness of life. There are real dangers which I may confront, and properly placed fear can keep me from walking into harm's way. But the fear of failing, of rejection, of the unknown, or of an imagined danger will cause me to limit my actions and miss the fullness of life.

The first step to conquering restrictive fears is to find what it is that frightens me. I might discover my fears through thoughtful analysis of my inaction. If quiet reflection does not do it, I can discuss the situation with a friend, who might offer insight. If my fear is severe enough to be classified as a phobia, through professional counselling it can be uncovered.

Once I have identified the object of my fear, the second step is to acquire as much knowledge as I can about it. Where did it originate? When did it begin? What is it stopping me from getting? I will find that the more knowledgeable I become, the less likely the fear will inhibit my actions.

The third step to overcoming fear is to concentrate on the benefit. Instead of focusing on the anticipated harm, I should consider what I lose by allowing it to limit my actions. If the benefit outweighs the risk, I will be compelled to move forward.

Finally, I can defeat fear by enhancing my self-esteem. The greater my belief in my potential for getting what I want, the more insignificant the fear of failing, being rejected, or suffering harm will appear to me.

****

Reflect also on: CONFORMITY, COURAGE, REJECTION.

HATRED

Hatred is powerfully destructive and can be defeated only with the omnipotence of love.

I have never started a fight, but I found myself involved in two during my school days. The first was while in the sixth grade. It was over an interest in a girl. The second was a couple of years later and was racially motivated. As I threw punches at Raymond in the sixth grade and at Paul in the eighth, I had one thing in mind: To inflict enough injury to get them to leave me alone. I acted in my best interest. I was driven by self-preservation. At the same time, I fought against theirs. The ill-will that I felt for both fellows was at those moments prompted by hatred. Love would not permit destroying another.

Upon reflection:

Hatred is a feeling of ill-will or malice toward another person. It is the absence of love. Hence, I cannot love and hate at the same time.

When hatred is the basis of my action, I create conflict in my life. That conflict expends energy that could be directed toward achieving the ultimate joy and success to which I am entitled. It is impossible for me to enjoy the fullness of life when I hate. That negative emotion leads me to thinking negatively toward the person I hate. Allowing negative thoughts to occupy my mind will surely affect the rest of what I think and believe.

The natural law of the universe requires

interaction with others. Beneficial interaction results from loving. When love is absent, relationships are impeded and/or destroyed. The law of the universe is then broken.

The destructive forces of this world such as crime, war, racism, and greed emanate from hatred. If I am governed by such forces, I will act to deprive someone else of the fullness and joy of life to further my own interests.

Hatred can creep in and permeate my life only if I refuse to love. If I commit an offense in hatred, I must immediately negate that act with an act of kindness. If hatred lingers, it will root itself and grow.

****

Reflect also on: LOVE, SELF-ESTEEM.

9

LIVING SKILLS

Through learning I expand my mind, broaden my horizons, and increase my options for success.

When you compare them by their potential risk and the likelihood of return, a compliment is a better investment than a criticism.

LEARNING

A degree may open doors, but learning opens the mind.

I was rendered totally blind by an accident at age four. However, an operation restored sight to the right eye. I gradually lost that sight over a period of twelve years.

Even after I noticed that the sight of my right eye was failing, I continued to read. I loved reading. To get enough light to see the print, I would either remove the lamp shade or set my book at the base of the lamp and stick my head underneath the shade. I strained my eye until I could no longer see to read. The last print that I saw was the headlines of the newspaper that read "Lee Harvey Oswald." I lost my dedication to reading when braille became my mode of written communication. My overall learning suffered as a result.

Upon reflection:

With a dedication to learning, I can enhance my knowledge and understanding of my world. Through learning I expand my mind, broaden my horizons, and increase my options for success.

Learning need not take place only in a formal educational setting. It began before I started school and continues today, long after I received an advanced college degree.

I can learn through a formal educational or training program. I can learn through reading books, magazines, and newspapers. I can learn from watching television or listening to the radio. I can learn from attending seminars or through conversations with another. All of these are ways by which knowledge can be transferred to me. But these are restricted means for learning. Moreover, the motive behind the sharing of thoughts and ideas may not have been for my edification but rather for the financial gain of someone else.

My immediate surroundings and current circumstances are my constant classroom. The teacher is I. If I pay attention, I can learn from my experiences. Not only should I learn what has happened and how it happened, but I ought to seek to understand why it happened. From this knowledge will come ideas and beliefs that will help me to understand my universe and will strengthen my control over my life.

****

Reflect also on: EXPERIENCES, KNOWLEDGE.

COMMUNICATE

An open mind and open ears are needed to communicate effectively.

Jacqueline and I met over the telephone on September 13, 1982. Not only did we talk for about an hour that day, but we had daily one-hour conversations. I learned much about her in a few days and knew that she was someone that I wanted to get to know better.

Our first date was to Las Vegas five days after we met. Travelling by bus from Los Angeles, we had six hours each way to talk together. That weekend provided sufficient information for me to know that I wanted a lifetime of talk with Jaci. I asked her to marry me only eight days after our first date. I also learned that we could communicate and I was certain that our marriage could last.

Upon reflection:

I cannot develop and sustain meaningful relationships with friends, kin, or colleagues if I cannot communicate. Love between two is meaningless unless communicated. Partners cannot successfully operate a business if they cannot express themselves freely to each other. Efficient management and work without conflict demand effective communication--that is, open, clear, two-way exchange.

Whenever I am required to interact with another person, I must be able to communicate successfully with that individual. That is, I must be able to share my thoughts and my feelings and to listen as someone else expresses him- or herself.

To effectively communicate is more than an ability to transmit my ideas or opinions. If I am to be a skillful communicator, I must also listen and understand. I must focus not on what I want to say but on what the other person is ready to hear. Moreover, I must allow equal time for listening.

As I listen to others, I will learn what to say and how to express it to get my idea across. I will gain information that will help me to formulate new ideas or to change those I have.

To be an effective communicator I must restrain my tongue and develop the patience to listen. As I engage in dialogue, I must be concise in expressing my opinions. I ought not monopolize the conversation. By pausing after a couple of minutes of speaking, I give my listener his or her opportunity to talk. When I ask questions, I invite others to express themselves.

****

Reflect also on: COMMUNICATION, COMPLIMENT, CRITICISM, GRATITUDE.

COMPROMISE

A compromise is the pliable intertwining of the interests of two people to strengthen the efforts of both in getting what they want.

As an attorney I represented a mother in her child custody matter. We offered a joint custody arrangement with the father for the two-year-old child. The father and his attorney refused. The father wanted full and complete custody, with the mother having limited visitation rights.

The matter was referred to a child psychologist for evaluation. The psychologist determined that in order for the child to get the benefit of interaction with both parents, he should be placed with his mother. His father was too much against the mother's input to have him as the custodial parent.

The father and his attorney were very willing to work out a compromise on child custody when we appeared in court after the psychological evaluation.

Upon reflection:

Because I am an individual with my own desires and goals, there are occasions when mine conflict with those of another. If I am to have meaningful relationships with other people and benefit from those relationships as I seek the joy and success of life, I must be willing and able to compromise. This is especially true when the relationship is one that requires constant and close interactions, such as in my marriage, as a parent, or in business.

My willingness to compromise stems from altruism and respect for others. It is rooted in my belief that there is a point at which I can have the desires of my heart and, at the same time, act in the best interest of others. Thus, the objective of compromise is to find that win-win situation.

To find that point of mutual best interest, I and the person with whom I am dealing must be able to communicate openly and honestly. We must commit ourselves to achieving what is best for both. Without such communication and commitment, there can be no compromise.

To compromise is not to sacrifice my wishes and aspirations. When I have reached an agreement, I must feel and believe that I am still on the path to getting what I want. A feeling that I have given up something that I deeply desire will fester into resentment. I cannot experience the fullness of life with resentment in my heart.

****

Reflect also on: ALTRUISM, RESPECT.

GRATITUDE

Unless you are a turkey, you should want Thanksgiving to be every day.

Jaci has done a fine job in teaching our four children to say thanks. "Please" and "thank you" were early words of their vocabularies. On their birthdays and at Christmas, she helps them to make lists of the people from whom they receive gifts. To each one they write a note to say thanks.

Upon reflection:

Throughout the year there are days which are designated for showing appreciation. In May we show our appreciation for mothers and in June, fathers. We honor a person on his or her birthday and express gratitude by giving a gift on Christmas. It is common that our appreciation is expressed by giving something material.

Thanksgiving is the one day of the year set aside to show gratitude, the expression of which need not be material. It is the time to say thanks when just the word is adequate. It is the opportunity to give a gift that I can keep for myself--giving thanks. It is the chance to thank God as well as the people around me for the benefits that I have received.

I can replicate the warmth and joy of giving thanks by showing gratitude every day. I can thank my wife for being a part of my life. For being understanding. I should thank my sons and daughters for doing well in school. For helping with household chores. I can tell the office support staff how much I appreciate their excellent performance. For reliable attendance.

I ought not let a day go by without expressing thanks--in a prayer, on the telephone, by sending a card or letter. When I find it hard to express appreciation face-to-face, I can do so in writing. I can take advantage of technology and send a facsimile or leave a message on E-mail or voice mail. A simple message such as "Thanks for responding immediately to my request" can make a great impact--and costs me nothing extra.

Showing my gratitude to another is one of life's mutually beneficial acts. I will feel good having done it, and the recipient of my gesture will be honored in receiving it.

****

Reflect also on: COMPLIMENTS, CRITICISM, GIVING.

LOVING

It is more likely the power of love and not the pain from its absence that frightens us into limiting our exposure to it.

As the chairman of the board, Peggy invited me, the executive director of the Disabled Resources Center, to lunch to discuss business. I was surprised, then, that she started with this advice: Find a woman who does not need you and you will be certain to find one that loves you.

I was twenty-eight years old at the time and wanted very much to share my life with a wife. By the time of Peggy's advice, I had asked six women (at different times) to marry me and had been engaged to five of them.

I found the advice to be good. I stopped dating women who seemed to depend on me. I looked for those who were independent. Jaci was the first to meet the new standard.

Upon reflection:

Loving is not dependence. The latter is an attempt to compensate for feelings of inadequacy. Loving is not just words or physical activity. These are futile efforts to express what one feels. Loving goes beyond mere feeling.

To love someone is to recognize that my enjoyment and fulfillment of life is intertwined with that of the loved one. It is to commit my soul, mind, and body to positive interaction with her or him to ensure our mutual benefit of what life offers.

Loving manifests itself through my ability to give. I show love when I can freely give of myself--soul, mind, and body. It is manifested when I give to another my positive thoughts and feelings. It is demonstrated when I can place a loved one's best interest in priority over my things.

My loving is also demonstrated through my willingness to forgive. If I am wronged by another person, I can unhesitatingly accept her or his repentance and continue to love. If I interact with others in love, I cannot hold a grudge or seek revenge. Such feelings of ill-will cannot exist simultaneously with love.

By loving I can control the flow of the positive and repel the negative forces of life. This is not to say that loving is my immunity against the injury and pain of negativism, but it is the source of healing and relief from the pain.

****

Reflect also on: ALTRUISM, GIVING, LOVE.

CRITICISM

It is the acceptance of criticism and not the offer that will lead to change for the better.

Being the church's youth leader, I was asked by the director of the youth choir what I thought of the day's rehearsal. Before I had a chance to respond, she said, "Never mind," and walked away.

I caught up to her to inquire why she did not want to hear my comments. I insisted that they would be given with the intent to encourage. She responded that she had never heard anything good from me concerning their singing. "You always criticize." This revelation gave me concern, and I realized that she was right. I criticize much more than I compliment. I wanted very much to undo that negative image of me.

Upon reflection:

Criticism is a tool that can be used both to build and to destroy. Even with my best intentions, the result might be the worse.

There are guidelines that I can follow to ensure that my critical comments will be constructive instead of destructive.

1. Never criticize one from whom I cannot take criticism. My offer of comment might be construed as an invitation to be criticized.

2. Never offer criticism where it is not invited.

Just because I see room for improvement does not mean that the person has an interest in or is ready to occupy that space.

3. Never pile on criticism. If I see a number of areas where a person can improve, I should identify for him or her only one or two of them. I may otherwise cause a person to feel that there is no hope for betterment.

4. Offer my comments as though I am the focus of the area of weakness. Instead of saying "You did not enunciate your words", I can say "I had trouble understanding some of your words".

5. Give compliments. Not only should I include with my critical evaluation positive comments, but from time to time I ought to give compliments without criticism. By so doing, I can avoid the perception that every time I open my mouth something negative will come out.

****

Reflect also on: COMPLIMENTS, ENCOURAGEMENT.

GIVING

The platinum rule is this: Give to others what you want them to give back to you.

In 1987, I appeared as a contestant on the game show $100,000 Pyramid. In the preliminary rounds, a category is selected and one must name seven items based on the description by one's partner. The title of the category is a hint to the common thread in the answers. In the bonus round a list of items is given, and one must identify their common elements in order to guess the category.

When I played the bonus round, I correctly guessed only four of six categories. For one category that I missed, my celebrity partner listed money and old clothes. I responded with "things that are faded", "things that are wrinkled", and "things that are torn". After my one minute had expired and the game was over, the game show host added one more item. He said, "blood". I blurted the correct answer, "Things that are donated (or given)".

Upon reflection:

The Christmas season is a well-known time for giving, but even those who do not follow the teachings of Christ have in their culture a celebrated time for gift exchange. One's generosity may be demonstrated several times during the year. Valentine's Day, Mother's Day, and Father's Day are special days for giving. I honor a friend or relative by giving gifts on the anniversary of his birth or her marriage. I need no special occasion to donate money, clothes, blood, or time to a nonprofit or charitable organization.

My giving does not end with tangible gifts. To show my appreciation I give thanks and to encourage another I give compliments. I may give advice or criticism to edify a friend. Values such as commitment, honesty, and respect have as their core the act of giving.

The act of giving is a universal law, both physically and spiritually. It is as vital to the life of my relationships with other people as oxygen is to the life of my body. If I end all my giving, sit around and wait to receive, or take without returning, I would see the significance of giving in my dealings with people. I would witness the decline of my friendships, the ineffectiveness of my networks, and the loss of the support I get from others. In other words, if I stop giving, others will stop giving to me.

****

Reflect also on: COMPLIMENTS, GRATITUDE, LOVING.

COMPLIMENTS

When you compare them by their potential risk and the likelihood of return, a compliment is a better investment than a criticism.

I bought my first house in April 1980 when mortgage interest rates were relatively high. To help me make the monthly payments, I invited one of my sisters and her family to live with me. With my paying for the house, my sister paid the utilities and bought the food. She also cooked. The latter was particularly beneficial for me, at the time a bachelor.

One day my sister prepared an absolutely scrumptious meal of roast and potatoes, cabbage, and cornbread. It was not easy for me to give a verbal compliment, so I wrote a letter. Recognizing the rarity of the praise, my sister vowed to frame it.

Upon reflection:

It is a good feeling to be complimented. A word of praise massages the human need for approval and acceptance. Even though I am uneasy when my accomplishments are recognized and honored, I like the showing of appreciation. I feel good that someone noticed my appearance and found it pleasing, or that my work was recognized and thought to be remarkable.

Compliments are encouraging. They give me the impetus to continue doing what I am doing because it is pleasing to others or because I am accomplishing what I desire.

Recognizing the joy of receiving compliments, I should be quick to show my appreciation of others and what they do. Every day I should find someone to compliment about something. At home I can praise my children for a good grade, good behavior, or a good effort. I can tell my wife how much I appreciate her being around. I can compliment the neighbor for the upkeep of his yard. I can express my appreciation for the work that my coworkers do that makes my job easier and/or my output better. I can write to the hotel manager to compliment the service I received, or I can leave a note for the person who provided the service. I can call a television or radio station to express my appreciation for a program aired.

Praise is a positive way of discouraging negative behavior. I can dissuade my wife from wearing the cologne that I do not like by repeatedly complimenting her when she wears the one I like. To praise the desired behavior is far better than criticizing the unwanted.

When they come from someone else, compliments are healthy for the mind and soul. Self-praise fattens the ego but thins out the crowd of those who might otherwise offer an expression of appreciation.

****

Reflect also on: CRITICISM, ENCOURAGEMENT, GIVING, GRATITUDE.

COMMUNICATION

Your communication is successful when you effectively engage the thoughts and feelings of your listener.

I first joined Toastmasters International in 1988. Though I had been speaking to youth in churches and students in schools, I gained a great deal about how to communicate successfully through my membership in Toastmasters.

I joined Toastmasters to better my use of gestures and to improve my ability to include humor in my speeches. The latter is essential to good public speaking because, as Mary Poppins advised, "a spoonful of sugar helps the medicine go down".

Upon reflection:

In my infancy, communicating was simple. I cried to get what I wanted. However, as I matured I learned other means of communicating--speech, writing, body language. I began to ask questions and to express my opinions. I discovered communication devices--microphone, book, telephone, radio, television, computer. I began to understand vulnerability and rejection. Now communicating is more complex.

If I am to be successful in business or employment and happy in my personal relationships, I must develop the skill of communicating in my complex environment.

First I must know my message. What do I want to convey? Each time that I express my ideas or my feelings, I am sharing aspects of my own identity. Knowledge of my message is the basis for self-confidence.

Second, I must organize my thoughts and opinions and understand my emotions. An organized presentation gives the listener a map to my ultimate message. It ensures that I am clear and concise. With organized ideas I can avoid rambling, a sign of uncertainty and insecurity.

Third, I must know the response I intend from my listener. With such knowledge I can determine the best method of communicating and which device to use. For instance, if I want to know the immediate reaction as opposed to a contemplative one, I must telephone rather than send a letter. If I want to be sure that my complete idea is considered, I should write.

Fourth, I must get feedback. To know if the message was conveyed, I must listen for the response.

When I listen to recordings of my speeches, I place myself in the position of the listener and I can discover if what I intended to say is what the audience heard. By listening, I learn ways to enhance the message and improve my style and delivery. I get useful evaluations of my presentations from members of my Toastmasters club.

****

Reflect also on: COMMUNICATE.

10

PRINCIPLES OF SUCCESS

That innate power to succeed is yet within me. I need merely to unleash my potential.

Those who persevere are not immune to failure or exempt from rejection but are undaunted by them.

SUCCEED

If your mind is not set to succeed, you leave the possibility of your success to chance; chances are that you will fail.

Michelle, seven years my junior, and I engaged ourselves in a friendly legalistic debate on a hypothetical problem. She had already expressed to me her desire and plan to attend law school. I thought I would give her a little moot court preview.

After Michelle made her argument, I began mine. "Suppose that ..."

Michelle held firmly that the hypothetical situation could never occur and that it was pointless to suppose such. In response to her insistence, I said harshly, "If you cannot put yourself in the situation to make the argument, you will never succeed in law school."

I regretted having made the pronouncement when Michelle informed me that she failed her first year of law school. I wonder from time to time if my negative assertion impacted her efforts.

Upon reflection:

There is within each of us an innate capacity to succeed. The dimensions of this ability are determined by instinct for survival, knowledge, power of will, and love. Working together, these elements will inevitably result in my getting what I want and finding joy in what I get.

The force of my power to succeed, however,

is weakened by negativism--words and/or experiences that I permit to quench my desire, deflate my confidence, suppress my will, and/or limit my imagination of and belief in the possibilities. A negative statement can cause me to lose the vision of my destination and to focus on the obstructions. By concentrating on the limitation, it becomes my expected result, and I will never work beyond my expectations.

That innate power to succeed is yet within me. I need merely to unleash my potential.

To release the power to succeed, my mind must be set for success. The foundation upon which it is set must be the belief that what I want to achieve can be done and the belief that I can do it. I must allow no room for doubt. My mind must be cleared of negativism. On this foundation of beliefs, I must build knowledge.

****

Reflect also on: BELIEFS, FAILURE, OBSTACLES, SUCCESS.

CONFIDENCE

When something comes to shake your confidence, stand on faith and hold onto hope.

There were several opportunities for me to apply for the position of presiding judge of the regional office where I work. I passed them all up. I thoroughly enjoy conducting hearings and writing decisions and did not want to leave that for managing a staff and answering to the chief judge. However, in an effort to keep all my options open, I submitted an application for presiding judge in 1995.

I entered the interview room with confidence. No, I was not confident that I would get the appointment as the presiding judge. Obtaining the appointment was subject to the will of the chief judge. But I had the confidence that I would reveal to the panelists exactly what I believed they should know about me and my abilities.

Upon reflection:

Confidence will push open doors that are closed. Confidence will get me through doors behind which others stand and block because they are uncertain of my abilities. When I speak and act with self-assurance, I invite others also to trust in me and my abilities.

To act with confidence is to exercise control. I must assume responsibility for my destiny. I ought never enter into a situation with the thought that my fate lies in the hands of another.

Though someone else may have the power to accept or reject me, it is only for that instance and not for life. To quit because of a failure or a rejection is to relinquish control. Confidence is the strength to turn failure and rejection from stumbling blocks to stepping stones.

If I believe in myself and my abilities, I will have confidence. I will remind myself as often as is necessary that I can and I will accomplish my objectives. Such reminder is necessary at least as frequently as disappointment or discouragement attempts to deter me from my goal. When I believe that I can, the resulting confidence will help me find the way.

Confidence thrives on knowledge. Always I must be aware of where I am and the direction in which I am going. I must know the steps that are needed to get what I want. When I am equipped with knowledge, I can move with confidence against the winds and words of opposition. With each successful step, I build even more confidence because I gain more knowledge of what I can successfully achieve.

****

Reflect also on: ABILITY, CAN, CONTROL, COURAGE.

VISION

Even on a clear day, your view of the world is dim when your vision is impaired.

I was not born blind. When I was four years old, I fell on the back of my head and split it open. I was rushed to the hospital where the doctors stitched up my wound and sent me home. My mother discovered that I could not see after observing me bump into walls and furniture. Upon examination, the doctors discovered that I suffered detached retinas.

About a year after my fall, I had an operation which restored sight to my right eye. With it alone, I read regular print while attending first grade. For second grade I had to read large print as the sight in the right eye began to deteriorate. Over a period of twelve years, I became completely blind again in that eye.

Upon reflection:

"Where there is no vision, the people perish:" wrote Solomon. [Proverbs 29:18] And his message is no less true today. Political leaders cannot govern without vision. The chief executive officer of a corporation cannot direct without vision. Nor can I reach my destination of success without vision.

Perfect vision is five dimensional. I first must keep a prospective view of my life. I must be able to look ahead to see clearly my goal and the road that leads to it. I must look ahead and see hope, instead of despair. My prospective view is complemented with circumspection, retrospection, and introspection.

Circumspection. I must be able to look at the present circumstances and find my opportunities. Without a keen sense of the opportunity that lies in the circumstances, I will be able to see only adversity.

Retrospection. I must be able to review my past and learn from my experiences. If I do not look back, I am likely to make the same mistakes of yesterday.

Introspection. I must be able to look within to know my thoughts and understand my feelings. I must look at myself and see purpose of life, instead of worthlessness.

If I can pick out the positive in the midst of the bleak, my vision is keen. I dare say, on the other hand, that I am blind if I see only darkness all around.

If my life is enveloped in darkness that limits my ability to look ahead, look around, look back, or look within, I can find the light of hope if I look up. The sure-fire test that I have the vision that will guide me through life is my ability to see God.

****

Reflect also on: FOCUS.

ENCOURAGEMENT

Encouragement is the mutual benefit of those who support one another; to get it, you must give it.

Two of the best assistants whom I have had to work for me in my capacity as an administrative law judge moved on from the job of reading and driving to higher pursuits. One became a special education teacher and the other, a personnel administrator. They both were high on skills but low on self-esteem. With one, it was not so much what I said that encouraged her. Rather, it was the example she saw in what I did. She independently made the decision to leave working for me to pursue her career.

To the other I gave much advice. The decision that forced her to seek other employment was made by me. I chose not to take her with me when I moved on to a different job.

I am encouraged with my having been instrumental in their achieving success.

Upon reflection:

How do I prepare myself for disappointment, which is bound to come? How can I insolate myself from the discouragement that would compel me to quit? I can maintain for myself a continual source of encouragement by mingling with those who are accomplishing what they want and by avoiding people who are negative.

There is no limit to the number of people who would offer advice, and no end to the occasions for which it would be offered. But all of it is not encouraging. I must be selective as to the voices to which I will listen.

First, I have to listen to the prompting of the inner voice. The one that speaks from within is my best source of encouragement because he knows my desires and is aware of what I am really capable of doing.

Next, I must listen to the voice of reason. When advice is given, I should test it for its consistency with what I believe to be truth and reality.

Never should I listen to the voice of doom. It most often echoes from the souls of the disheartened, who themselves need encouragement.

Since actions speak much louder than words, I can be certain that my encouragement can surely come from those who are doing what I want to do. From this group I should choose my friends and associates.

****

Reflect also on: ASSOCIATION, BEGINNINGS, DESPAIR, FRIENDSHIP, SUPPORT.

INITIATIVE

When you take the initiative to act in your best interest, you become the perpetrator instead of the victim of circumstances.

After completing high school, it would have been easy for me to sit on my duff and do nothing. I had blind classmates who opted for idleness.

The government labeled me as an individual who could not work due to blindness and was willing to send me a monthly check. The admissions committee of Yale was reluctant to admit me because they did not think I could handle the curriculum. The expectation of most employers--and indeed, most people--is that a blind person cannot do the work required of a "normal" employee. Even some family members asked why I bothered to go to college when I could sit at home and get a check. But I took the initiative and attended college and law school and found a job. I was determined to make things happen the way I thought they should happen.

Upon reflection:

If I want something done, let alone done right, I have to do it myself. I alone can act in my best interest. Though others may be willing to act on my behalf, in truth, they will do what is best for them. They will suppose that what is best for them is best for me.

The sun will rise, the wind will blow, and the earth will quake whether I want them to or not.

Over natural events I have no control. But knowing that sunshine and rain promote growth, I can plant a rosebush and enjoy the beauty and the fragrance that will naturally follow. In other words, by taking the initiative to act, I can benefit from things over which I have no control.

Other than natural events, things happen because people make them happen. I must, as others do, take the initiative to make things happen. Even if I am not certain what the outcome will be, I must put action to my plans.

I can make the circumstances of each day of my life be the circumstances that propel me to my goal. I cannot just sit and wait for things to happen. I must not wait for opportunity to come my way. I should create the opportunity. When I make excuses based on my situation, I rob myself of the verve for taking initiative.

****

Reflect also on: ACTION, DRIVE.

RESOLVE

Resolve brings reality to dreams by transforming desire into determination.

The recruiter from Princeton asked me which college was my first choice. I told him that it was Yale. The idea of going to Yale started with a joke in my U.S. History class but was encouraged by my friend Harvey, who had been accepted a year before. Once I decided that Yale was where I would go to school, nothing could shake me on that issue.

Yale initially did not consider my application. But I received acceptances from Stanford, Columbia, Princeton, and the Massachusetts Institute of Technology. I still was determined to get into Yale.

Upon reflection:

I can never realize my dreams with desire alone. Either I wish and want and wait for good fortune to chance my way, or I wrest my destiny from the hands of happenstance and resolve to have my desires satisfied. The latter is the way of certainty.

Desire is just the first step to my success. Once I know what I want, I must decide to get it.

I must not be afraid to say without reluctance "I will do it" or "I will get it". I cannot let thoughts of impossibility dash my hopes. Just because no one else has done it or just because it is going to take time or just because it costs money that I do not have is no reason to not be resolute to have what I want.

My decision to see my dream realized is the foundation of my determination. I must then determine the course that leads to my goal. It may be that I will follow a course of education. Perhaps I need to seek financial backing for my idea. Sometimes it is just a matter of waiting for the right time. Resolve will set me on the right course.

My resolve is manifested in a plan of action. In formulating my plans, I must set my ultimate goals and preliminary objectives. I have to develop a time frame for achieving those goals and objectives. The absence of a plan of action is indicative of indecision and a weak resolve.

****

Reflect also on: COMMITMENT, DETERMINATION, DRIVE.

DETERMINATION

Determination can change adversity to advantage and obstacles to opportunities.

When Anton was two years old, he was determined to go outside to play with his brother and sister. Jaci and I were determined to keep our third child inside so that we could keep an eye on him. No matter what we did to confine him, he discovered a way to get out. His stubborn determination is exhibited in every aspect of his life.

When he was just two and a half years old, Anton observed a dance class for children. He expressed a desire to dance. After the dance instructor told him that he could not be in the class until he was three years old, he said nothing more about it. Until he was three. When asked what he wanted for his birthday, Anton replied, "I want to dance." He has been dancing ever since.

Upon reflection:

With determination I can get what I want. Determination is the heart of perseverance and the fuel for drive. With determination I will know when to keep up the attack as I struggle toward my goal. Determination will direct me around or over the obstacles which lie in my way.

I must first know what I want. If the object of my pursuit is not the desire of my heart, the first sign of difficulty will be my excuse to quit. Determination cannot exist if not based on desire.

When the vision of my goal is clear, determination will find for me the best way to reach it. Barriers cannot break my will and pitfalls will not present peril. If the path that I travel does not lead to my dream, I can find an alternate route if I remain determined.

I cannot let discouragement erode my determination. I must separate myself from people who speak negativism instead of encouragement. A constant bombardment of debasing or dissuasive words can quench the fire that burns within.

Determination will not allow me to quit. When I feel like giving up, I should check the strength of my desire, measure the height of my self-esteem, reconsider the soundness of my belief that it is possible, and remind myself of the satisfaction that will come from achieving what I set out to do. This reexamination of my desire, self-esteem, and resolve will rekindle my determination.

****

Reflect also on: ENDURANCE, PERSEVERANCE, QUITTING, RESOLVE, WILL.

FOCUS

Life itself will be clear or dark depending on what is your focus.

I was nine years old when my mother took me to the ophthalmologist for an eye examination in preparation for the next school year.

The doctor asked, "Is it clearer or darker?" as he attempted to test my vision.

Even after repeating the question several times, I never answered. I did not know to what he referred. "Is what clearer? Is what darker?" I wondered. The doctor never told me on what to focus and I was too naive and afraid to ask. Who knows what treatment I missed because the examination was not completed?

Upon reflection:

To be my best at what I am doing or to give the most when I am giving, I must focus. I must be able to center my attention on the object of my activities. In other words, I must have a clear picture of what I am doing and know with no uncertainty why it is being done.

To focus is to direct my thoughts and concentrate my emotions on what I wish to accomplish. I must keep in the fore of my imagination a clear vision of where I want to be. Then, I have to collect my efforts and my activities and direct them toward my goal.

To maintain focus, I must consider each step

that I take and avoid acting out of habit. Habitual actions absent of focus will leave me vulnerable to distractions. I make mindless mistakes when I do not concentrate on what I am doing.

When I keep my objectives in focus, I will not be deterred by the inevitable problems and pain that can pillage my hope. When my mind is focused, I cannot be lured by impatience or indecision in a direction that does not lead to my goals.

When my destination is in focus, my determination will not falter. I will have before me a constant reminder of the purpose of my actions. I can move with boldness and confidence having no doubt as to where I am headed.

Having my destination constantly in focus, I can see the world through dream-colored glasses. I am able to view everything in the context of how it gets me to my goal.

****

Reflect also on: OPTIMISM, VISION.

QUITTING

The choice is this: Suffer for the moment the struggle of the journey or live forever with the defeat of quitting.

In August 1991, I made the decision to pursue professional speaking as a business. I met with early success in obtaining paid speaking engagements. And the joy I experience when addressing an audience is great. Yet, within two years of launching my new endeavor, I considered quitting. I telephoned my mentor and friend Joe Sweeney to let him know of my discouragement. I received from him no words of encouragement; just a sympathetic ear. A night of restful sleep after venting to Joe helped me to work out the problem. I awakened with a renewed commitment to succeed.

Upon reflection:

When I feel like quitting, I will check my desire. I have to take a fresh look at what it is that I want. If my desire to have what I am working toward is still strong, to quit just might be wrong.

When I feel like quitting, I will assess my resolve. I should think back to the moment when I made my decision to move toward my current goal. What were the reasons behind my decision? Are they yet valid? I should review the plans that I made to achieve my objectives. Are they still good? If my resolve is yet sure, I will try to endure.

When I feel like quitting, I will test my initiative. Why is it that I feel that I cannot take another step in the direction of my goal? If within me there is still fight, to quit would not be right.

When I feel like quitting, I will examine my vision. Am I looking carefully for the opportunity that exists in the present circumstances? Can I see the hope that is ahead? Or am I focusing on the obstacle that prompts me to quit? If my vision is clear, my success will appear; I will not quit.

When I feel like quitting, I will review the past. I will look at the things that I have been able to accomplish. I will consider the investment of time, effort, and money that I have already made. If there has been success in the past, I surely can last.

When I feel like quitting, I will call a friend. I will share with him or her the despair, disappointment, or discouragement that I feel. If I still have a friend, I can get to the end.

****

Reflect also on: DETERMINATION, ENDURANCE, PERSEVERANCE.

BEGINNINGS

You can get the most out of life if you live each day with the energy and enthusiasm of a new beginning.

Partying to celebrate the coming of a new year has never been an activity of mine. Most invitations I turn down. I accepted one from friends in Compton to bring in 1990, but when Jaci and I arrived in the area, about six o'clock in the evening, the celebratory gun-shooting had already begun. We turned around and went back home.

Though I do not party, I engage in the common practice of making new-year resolutions. Throughout the day on December 31, I reflect on the out-going year, considering things that I wanted to do but did not. I think about things that I did and wished that I had not. As midnight approaches, I begin a mental process of promising to myself how the new year will be different. But as the year wears away, so do the promises.

Upon reflection:

The beginning of a new year brings energy, fresh promises, and encouragement with a sense of new hope. To succeed and to enjoy the fullness of life, I need such a revival more often than once a year.

Each time that I awaken from a restful night's sleep, my body is revitalized with energy for the day's activities. My mind is clear for fresh thoughts and new ideas. The setting is ripe for the encouragement of a new hope if I am willing to honor the in-coming of January 2 and 3 and 4 and each day of the rest of the year as I celebrate January 1. Each day to which I awaken is the beginning of new life.

I should begin each day with new resolutions. The content may be the same as those of yesterday, but today's resolve is a new one because there is a renewed commitment to it.

When I make my vows, I can commit myself to shorter segments of time instead of making them for a year. If I resolve to stop being critical of others, for instance, I can make my promise for one day. If I break my promise, the next day will give me the opportunity for a fresh start. When I keep my vow, I will find strength of will to repeat my successful action.

To help me keep my resolve, it is necessary that I set myself up for success. If, for example, I promise myself to lose weight, I must change the circumstances of my eating and exercise habits. I must remove from my reach the foods I should avoid and change my schedule of daily activities to comfortably include time to exercise. The alterations in my surroundings and my time schedule will give me a true sense of a new beginning.

I must not forget to wipe the slate clean at the end of the day. I will encounter disappointments and failures. But I should never dwell on these. I will remember them only long enough to draw lessons and to make modifications to tomorrow's plans.

****

Reflect also on: ENCOURAGEMENT, HABIT.

ENDURANCE

Until the goal is reached, you cannot know your capacity to endure.

My first year at Yale was a lonely and depressing one. It was my first time leaving home, and I was three thousand miles away from my high-school friends. I spent many a day in my dormitory room listening to the mournful songs of Roberta Flack. Even today listening to "First Take" conjures up the pain of those morose college days.

I never once considered leaving Yale, though I was unhappy. I had to stay to prove to the school administration that a blind person could handle Yale's curriculum. If I had quit, I might have ruined opportunities for other sightless students. And it would not have been for academic reasons. Hence, I endured the loneliness and depression to achieve the success that I knew would come.

Upon reflection:

To endure is to set my goal, start my course, and go until I am satisfied. If my desire for the object is weak, I will lack the fervor that is necessary to get me through times of stress or struggle. I will be disheartened by the slightest set back. But when my desire is strong, I will find the way to get to what I want.

To endure is to make a decision and carry my plans to the finish. If I am indecisive and unsure about the direction of my efforts, confusion will zap me of determination. A firm decision is the foundation of courage. I can build on that foundation a fortress against the defeat that results from quitting.

To endure is to initiate action and keep the momentum going until my goal is reached. If I lose my initiative, I stop making things happen. When things do not happen, I cannot last. A sustained initiative will get me over the hurdles to success. Idleness, on the other hand, is the forerunner to quitting.

To endure is to see my way past the obstacles and over the pitfalls encountered on the road to success. If I cannot see opportunity in adverse circumstances, the inevitable challenges of life will defeat me. Clear vision will lead me to where I want to be. When I maintain focus, I can endure.

****

Reflect also on: DRIVE, PERSEVERANCE, QUITTING.

PERSEVERANCE

Those who persevere are not immune to failure or exempt from rejection but are undaunted by them.

I am not ashamed to tell people that I did not pass the California Bar Exam on my first try. Given the passage rate, a good percentage of those who take the exam do not pass on the first attempt. I took a bar review course, traveling alone by bus at night to attend the class sessions. I did a fair amount of studying. Yet, I failed.

From taking the exam the first time I learned what changes I needed to make in order to better my chance at passing. I petitioned the Committee of Bar Examiners for an additional fifteen minutes for the multiple choice questions. Having the 100 questions (for each session) read aloud took extra time. I was unable to get to seven questions in the first Multistate session. Although I failed the exam on the second attempt with enough time to answer the questions, I persevered. I tried again because I knew that I had the knowledge and ability to pass and I would not let the exam defeat me.

Upon reflection:

Often I will find myself struggling to get what I want. I just have to remember to keep moving ahead. It is perseverance that will pay off. So long as I am certain of what I want to have or wish to be, I should tenaciously pursue it to the end.

Perseverance requires that I continue to act.

I cannot diminish my effort in the face of uncertainty. I must strengthen my resolve.

I cannot quit when I encounter obstacles or barriers but must find a way to overcome or get around them.

I must not despair in the midst of failure or rejection. I have to try again.

I need not continue the same approach in order to persevere. Butting my head against the wall will hurt. I should learn from my experience and avoid that pain. I can persevere toward my goal but change my approach. When someone rejects my idea, I should keep searching for one who will accept it. If today someone tells me no, I can ask again at another time and I may get the answer I wish.

Perseverance requires that I walk the tight rope between persistence and annoyance. A squeaky wheel can either get the grease, resulting from persistence, or get changed, from annoyance. I can be persistent without being unpleasant if I am sensitive to the response from others.

****

Reflect also on: CHALLENGE, DETERMINATION, DRIVE, ENDURANCE, WILL.

11

REVIVING THE SOUL

I cannot subtract years and I will not revive the body of my childhood. But I can regain the spiritual innocence of my youth.

The success of prayer will come when I have established the way to make direct and continuous contact with God.

REJUVENESCENCE

The youthfulness of the soul that is lost in the toils of life is found again through rejuvenescence.

During the summer after my first year of law school, I worked for the Los Angeles City Attorney. Instead of the research that most first-year law students performed as summer employment, I answered the telephone calls from the thousands of people living in Los Angeles who thought the City Attorney was an attorney for anyone residing in Los Angeles. I handled an average of forty-seven calls a day, listening to complaints and name-calling, the likes of which cannot be printed in this volume.

After two months, the pressure got to me. I yelled "shut up" at a caller who would not take a breath for me to give her the advice she sought. I felt awful about losing my temper. I had not allowed myself a time of mental and spiritual renewal from the constant bombardment of complaints and name-calling.

Upon reflection:

The pressure will get to me. The customers' complaints. The boss's demands. The children fighting. My being treated unfairly. My not getting the recognition that I deserve. My being called names. It happens daily and it can get to me if I do not find for myself the time for recreation, refreshing my mind, and renewing my spirit.

Rejuvenescence is the renewal of youthfulness.

I cannot subtract years and I will not revive the body of my childhood. But I can regain the spiritual innocence of my youth. The innocence that allows a free imagination to roam the universe of creativity. The innocence that has no inhibitions about trying new things. I can revive the mental capacity that knew nothing about impossibility and was not thwarted by fear.

Rejuvenescence takes place when I find the time and place for quietude. For listening to my inner voice. It happens when I turn off the television and open this volume of inward reflections. I may be rejuvenated by listening to motivational or inspirational speakers or by attending a spiritual fellowship. I must discover the means for my soul's revitalization.

****

Reflect also on: PRAYER, QUIETUDE.

QUIETUDE

When you understand that talk is cheap and silence is golden, it is easy to figure which will bring the greatest wealth.

I have, since my youth, always been an early morning person. I got up as early as five o'clock in the morning to go to school. In college my studies did not get done if not before noon. Now that I am married and have a houseful of children, the early morning hours are my favorite. It is then that I find the most quiet. Whether I lie in bed for a moment or sit at the computer, my thoughts flow freely, new ideas are born, and problems are solved. I reflect on yesterday and plan my activities for the day.

Upon reflection:

My pursuit of success and the fullness of life is one that can keep me rather busy. In the hustle and bustle of the day's activities my ears are continuously assaulted by the conversation of others, the noise of traffic, the television, the radio, or the stereo. To maintain health and balance, I must find time for quietude. It must be quiet time other than when I am sleeping.

Quietude is a state of rest and tranquility for all of me, my eyes and ears as well as my muscles. I find a place where I can sit or lie comfortably, close my eyes, and appreciate silence. It does not matter what time of day I find for my time of stillness. When I can achieve such calm while awake, I gain more rest and rejuvenation from my sleep. Moments of stillness are important for physical, mental, and spiritual health.

In my quiet moments I can listen to the softness of the voice that utters from within. He will tell me more about myself. He will explain my feelings, stimulate my thoughts, and encourage my imagination.

My creativity sprouts and my dreams are born in quietude. When I shut out the sights and sounds of my physical environment, my mind and spirit are released to move beyond human limitations.

****

Reflect also on: DREAM, IMAGINATION, PRAYER.

BALANCE

Learn to live with balance and you can avoid living on the edge.

My wife and I took our four children to spend nine days in Hawaii. I realized during that trip that the four-year lapse of time with no family vacation was too long. I made a commitment to take the family on an extended vacation at least once every two years.

While in Hawaii, I spent my time simply enjoying the break from the pressures of work. It was an opportunity to read, listen, and write. I felt good about doing something other than the constant hurry-up-and-get-it-done routine of the job.

Upon reflection:

My success is meaningless if to get there I push myself into a state of ill health, either mentally or physically, or both. I cannot enjoy the abundance of life if I do not regard all elements of it. My life cannot be full unless I cater to the needs of body, mind, and soul. There must be a balance that keeps the three in appropriate interaction.

I cannot allow myself to become so enslaved to making another dollar that I am unable to enjoy the freedom of relaxation. If I allow myself the necessity of leisure, my health and quality of work will be enhanced. I must take time off from work. Spending time on the job or at a business is an economic necessity and not a law of nature.

I should change my environment by taking a vacation. It does not have to be far or long. The importance is the change in surroundings. I should get away from the familiar stimuli--the uncut grass, the full trash can, the unopened mail--that pushes me into my daily routine. The change will permit me to engage in new activities. A difference in scenery can provoke fresh thought.

Excess is the enemy of balance; moderation is its friend. I must take heed to not overdo. Watching too much television is as injurious to the mind as eating too much is harmful to the body. A steady diet of only TV news and sitcoms will do as much for mental health as a regular diet of only chocolate bars and soda will for my physical well-being.

To achieve balance in my life, I must engage in activities which feed and strengthen the mind and the soul just as I eat properly and exercise to maintain physical health. I must learn the basics of mental and spiritual nutrition and develop good habits to be sure to get the proper daily allowance of positiveness and love.

****

Reflect also on: TEMPERANCE.

PRAYER

Have a heart to heart talk with a friend but a spirit to spirit talk with God.

When I met Herb in the mid-seventies, he had graduated from college and, at twenty-nine years of age, was vice-president of the bank branch where he worked. He was high with excitement about his success. Contributing to his pride, no doubt, was the fact that he is an African-American and had achieved success despite the obstacles his ethnicity presented. I must admit, yet being a student in college, I was envious of him. That is, until I learned his position on God. He said, "I don't need God. I'm doing quite well without him. If I get to the point that I need his help, I'll call on him."

Unlike Herb, most people whom I have met follow some religious doctrine. Despite the differences in religions which they represent, all have a way to communicate with the supernatural being who is the focus of their faiths. They all pray.

Upon reflection:

I need not be religious to pray. Prayer is the communication that takes place between my inner being--that is, my soul--and the supernatural force of the universe. It is a spirit to spirit exchange.

Because prayer is a spiritual exchange, it does not matter in what position I place my body. I can bow my head. I can raise my hands and look upward. I can kneel, face the east, or place my body in a meditative contortion. Nor does it matter the time that I pray. By its very nature, the Supreme Being is attentive at all times. The establishment of a ritual, including physical posture as well as time, is important as a reminder to focus on communication with God.

The success of prayer will come when I have established the way to make direct and continuous contact with God. There are no magical words with which to pray. Verbal language is merely a physical communication device. The words and/or thoughts that direct my focus on God are the ones that I should use.

If it is not a two-way exchange, my prayer is incomplete. It must include moments of stillness and quietude in order for God to talk to me.

Given the talents and abilities bestowed on me when I was created, there is much that I can accomplish without directly communicating with God. However, there is much more that is possible for me when I am in contact with the Omnipotent.

****

Reflect also on: GOD, RELIGION, SPIRITUALITY.

RELIGION

What purpose does religion serve if it seeks to nurture the essence of your soul through conformity and fear?

For twenty years I was a member of a Pentecostal church. I was an active member. Then in 1978, though I did not join as a member, I worked with a nondenominational congregation. After a year of service, I was invited to be the pastor of the church. I declined. From 1982 to the present, my membership has been with Baptist congregations, though in that period I have attended the services of Lutherans, Methodists, Presbyterians, and several other denominations. I have been recruited by the Mormons, the Jehovah Witnesses, and the Nation of Islam. I have learned that they all purport to know God and each has the one and only way to reach him.

Upon reflection:

I seek to know God, the supreme force of the universe. It is through my soul that I can interact with Him. Because my soul was created by God and emanates from Him, I yearn to be connected with Him. Religion is meaningful to my experiencing the fullness of life only when it serves to feed and nurture my soul with the love of God.

Having my name placed on the membership roll of a particular congregation will not join my soul to God. Regular attendance of church services does not connect me with the presence of God. Enthusiastic participation in the activities of the church is not interaction with the power of God. Strict adherence to the doctrine of my religious denomination will not ensure eternity with God.

The only way that I can feel the presence of God and share in His omnipotence is to open my soul to His love. The love of God is eternal, universal, and unconditional.

If my soul and mind are permeated by love, my actions will reflect love. I will not need a list of dos and don'ts to govern my behavior. Love will control.

If I am connected through love with God, it does not matter what name I assign to my spiritual doctrine. Love has no religion. It does matter, however, that my religion allows me the freedom to interact with God. If instead it induces fear and imposes conformity, religion contravenes God's love because there is no fear in love. There are no conditions to God's love.

I reverence God when I exemplify His never-ending love to all. If I am unable to so love, there is no worship in the song that I sing or the praise that I give to Him. There is no spiritual value in the dedication I show to my church if my life itself does not reflect God.

****

Reflect also on: CONFORMITY, FAITH, GOD, MORALITY, PRAYER, SOUL, SPIRITUALITY.

12

PEOPLE WHO NEED PEOPLE

If I am altruistic, my selflessness will be demonstrated toward all because it is a characteristic of me and not an act that I perform.

Just as a romance cannot last if only one is in love, a friendship cannot exist through the efforts of one party.

INDEPENDENCE

True independence is being in control of self, the whole self, and no one but self.

The white cane is a symbol of independence to a person with a visual impairment. With its use, a sightless child can let go the hand of her parent; a blind man need not hold the elbow of his companion.

I first learned to use the cane at age fifteen. In mobility training I was not only taught the proper techniques for holding and moving the cane, but I learned to ask for help. Once I started using it, the range of my independent activities saw no bounds. I could ride the bus on my own, traveling to locations where I had never been before. Such independence enabled me to visit and date Jaci when she was attending UCLA law school and was herself unable to drive.

Upon reflection:

When I am independent, I have the freedom to pursue my goals no matter where they might lead me. I can move forward with confidence that I can avoid peril and can hurdle obstacles that sit between me and what I want. Independence is freedom from worries about what lies in the future.

To be independent does not require that I dissolve my marriage or get rid of my children. Independence is not solitude, isolation, or loneliness. I can be independent and continue to love my family, enjoy my friends, and work with my colleagues.

When I am independent, I need not control another in order to feel important. The power that I experience is from self-control and not domination over another.

Independence is my knowing and pursuing the desires of my heart. It is my being in control of my destiny. It is my taking responsibility for where I am and what I am doing, instead of making excuses for my plight.

I am independent when I believe that there is life after the death of a loved one; that there is healing after tragedy; that there is happiness in the absence of possessions; that there is success after the loss of a job or business; that I have direct contact with the Supreme Spirit of the universe.

****

Reflect also on: CONTROL, DEPENDENCE, HELP.

MARRIAGE

You must pledge your soul, mind, and body if your marriage is to be a life-long experience.

Born in New Hampshire, Jaci grew up in Brooklyn, New York; I was born and reared in Compton, California. Jaci is an only child, while I am one of twelve. Jaci has a strong interest in music but has difficulty with math, and I am the opposite. Despite our differences, we had a common friend in Lynn. Learning of Jaci's plan to attend law school in California, Lynn gave her my telephone number. Jaci's first call to me on the evening of September 13, 1982, was the beginning of our sharing life together. We married nine months later.

Upon reflection:

Marriage is a promise between two individuals to live as one. The two do not become a single being but they are two sharing life and seeking its joy and fullness together. However, for my marriage to be successful, I must pledge my body, mind, and soul to the joint venture.

When I pledge my soul, I make love the binding emotion of my relationship. The stronger the love, the greater the chance that my marriage will last. It will withstand geographic separation and survive physical death. My ability to communicate is the key to love's continued development.

For my marriage to be strong, I must retain my identity while maintaining a sense of mutuality.

Thus, in pledging my mind to the union, I must promise to support and encourage my wife in the fulfillment of her dreams. I must think positive thoughts and hold powerful beliefs in my ability and hers to achieve the best that each is capable of achieving. Through compromise I can ensure our mutual benefit.

The pleasure of a physical relationship can only last as long as I do. Hence, a pledge of my body must be more than an offer to satisfy my partner's desires. It must also be a promise to maintain my body in good health. Caring for myself is key to keeping my relationship alive.

****

Reflect also on: COMMITMENT, COMMUNICATE, COMPROMISE, LOVE, LOVING.

FAMILY

People may be bound together through biology or by law, but love is what creates strong family ties.

My dad had three children, my mother had two, and they got together to have seven more. My twin sister and I are the oldest of the seven. At no time did the twelve children live together. Consequently, we have not been a tight family unit. In my college days, I described our family as being more akin to the original confederation than to the United States. However, as we have grown older, we recognize the benefits of strong family ties.

Upon reflection:

Life can be a tough journey at times, but I find that my family can help to make my trip an enjoyable one. My parents, siblings, wife, children, or other relatives can be a source of support. They can encourage, advise, and/or help me both in my career development and in my personal growth. But I cannot assume that such treasure source will be available simply because they have a biological or legal connection with me. The more important bond is of our souls.

My relationships with family members must be cultivated and nurtured just as those with friends. I cannot take my family for granted. If I do, the family ties may come undone. I cannot assume that my family will be supportive of me and will encourage me in the pursuit of my dreams. Sometimes the familial ties are so knotted as to be of no useful value.

While there are biological or legal ties that join me with a relative, I must seek to maintain independence. Dependent relationships cannot benefit me. I must maintain control of my life and mine alone. I have to let my family members carry the burdens of their own choices.

I should cultivate my family relationships with communication and understanding. If I cannot visit regularly with relatives, I can use the telephone or send a letter to keep in touch. My communications ought to involve the sharing of ideas, aspirations, and dreams, not just historical events.

I must nurture relationships with family members with love and support. Love will ensure that the bonds between my family and me are strong.

****

Reflect also on: MARRIAGE, SUPPORT.

ASSOCIATION

One's journey to success is made unnecessarily difficult by associating with those who prefer the path of failure.

My brother was an "A" student in high school until he started associating with a different group of so-called friends. He lost his interest in studying. They encouraged him to steal, the result being his incarceration in a juvenile detention facility. There he gained a different group of associates and his antisocial behavior continued.

My brother tried to clean up his act. Once while incarcerated, he wrote a letter to me asking if I would help him to change. He reasoned that since I was free and he was locked up, I must have been doing something right. But not until he parted company with wrongdoers did he stop doing wrong.

Upon reflection:

My decision to associate with an individual in business or as a friend is a tacit approval or endorsement of that person's conduct or life style. Such approval leads to assimilation. Hence, I must watch the company I keep.

There are plenty of people who will build me up and help me to succeed. I need not associate with those who will not. There is enough negativism that will occur from those who do not know me. I need not accept the negativism of family or so-called friends.

If I want to succeed, I must associate with

those who support success--theirs and mine. I must not cling to relationships with those who are failures. I must dissociate myself from the purveyors of doom. I must let negative family members know that their negativism interferes with my drive to succeed. When I tell them of my dislike of their negativism, I must do it tactfully or I too will be a negative individual.

A negative person can easily be identified. I can listen to the words of negativism and know that the behavior of the speaker will be concomitant. The weather is either too hot or too cold for her; never is it comfortable. The response to "how are you" is usually a complaint of fatigue or pain or the retort "I can't complain". The negative person comments only on the negative aspects of an event and finds humor only in the negative facets of life. When I associate myself with such negativism, I will begin to live it.

I cannot isolate myself from everyone. The fullness of life involves interaction with others. But I will associate myself with only those who also seek the fullness of life.

****

Reflect also on: FRIENDSHIP, NEGATIVISM, SUPPORT.

FRIENDSHIP

Financial gain or personal benefit may come from being well connected, but love and joy come from having a friend.

Rami is a friend. We met at Yale in 1971. Though we are separated by over a thousand miles and do not see each other often, our relationship has lasted and strengthened. We talk only two, sometimes three, times a year over the telephone. She calls me on my birthday, and I call her on hers. I listen to her successes in writing classical music, and she endures my stories about speaking. In the twenty-two years since I left Yale, we have seen each other in person only once. But the bond of our friendship is strong enough that she named her first child Arielle Dana.

Upon reflection:

A friendship begins with a shared interest that is often identified through a common association. I have friends whom I met in school, at church, on the job, in the neighborhood, and through membership in Toastmasters. Encountering another in these settings presented the opportunity to talk, and the development of the relationship began. But the common interest alone does not create the friendship and cannot sustain it.

Unlike familial ties, there is no biology or law which connects friends. The friendship bond is of voluntary commitment. If it is not adequately nur tured, a friendship will not last.

My relationship with a friend is fed by communicating with each other. It does not have to be often. A letter or a telephone call from time to time to stay in touch will sustain the relationship. The important thing is that I feel free to share with a friend my hopes and dreams. I too must be available to listen to a friend as she or he shares with me. I should be ready and willing to give encouragement or solace when it is needed.

A one-sided relationship is not a friendship. There must be mutuality. Just as a romance cannot last if only one is in love, a friendship cannot exist through the efforts of one party. Though I may sincerely wish to have a particular person as a friend, if my love is not being returned, I should turn my efforts elsewhere. I can continue my search for the relationship that is mutual.

****

Reflect also on: ENCOURAGEMENT, SUPPORT.

ALTRUISM

You demonstrate altruism when you respond with compassion where self-interest or society would dictate otherwise.

I did not become familiar with the term "altruism" until I was about twenty-five years old. The term was infused into my vocabulary by Dr. Martin Luther King, Jr.

To illustrate the concept of unselfish concern for another, Dr. King, in a sermon titled "Who Is My Neighbor", used the New Testament parable which is commonly known as the story of the Good Samaritan. The Samaritan defied conventional rules of society by having compassion for a person who was of a different ethnic group and less fortunate than he. The Samaritan administered first aid to, provided transportation for, and paid for the hospice of the victim of a mugging and robbery whom he found along the road. This he did after two religious leaders of the victim's own ethnic group ignored his plight as they passed him by. [Luke 10:30-37] Dr. King concluded with the message that my neighbor is anyone to whom I have the opportunity to be neighborly.

Upon reflection:

Can I do it? Can I put the needs of another before my own interests? Can I give up the material things for which I work so hard for the healing of an individual less fortunate than I? If the someone else is my immediate family member, the likelihood is that I can. But what if the someone else is a distant relative? A neighbor? A person of an ethnic group or nationality different from mine? When I can have and demonstrate compassion for a person outside my realm of commonality--that is, a stranger--I am altruistic.

Altruism is the unselfish interest in the well-being of others. My concern for others must be without the hope or expectation of return or gain; otherwise, it is not unselfish. I may receive and accept reward or recognition for my altruistic acts, but my deeds must be performed without anticipation of reward or recognition.

Altruism is a characteristic of my being manifested by my conduct toward others. As such, it is universal. I cannot be selective about the persons toward whom I am altruistic. The process of choosing one person over another to be the object of my good will requires the superimposition of my self-interests over the universe of those in need. In other words, when I pick and choose the individuals who are to benefit from my deeds, I am satisfying some element of self-interest. Hence, my good will is not altruism. It is favoritism. If I am altruistic, my selflessness will be demonstrated toward all because it is a characteristic of me and not an act that I perform.

****

Reflect also on: LOVING, RESPECT.

13

RIGHT TIME; RIGHT PLACE

My potential for success changes with every change in circumstances.

Whether or not the condition, situation, or set of circumstances with which you are faced is an adversity depends on how you look at it.

CIRCUMSTANCES

The circumstances may be by happenstance, but to be a victim of them is by choice.

Though I elected to attend college thousands of miles from home, I vowed to return to Compton, California, to make a contribution to the community in which I grew up. Keeping my promise, I bought my first house in my home town. I took great interest in the public schools, even before I had children who might one day be students in the system.

After a couple of unsuccessful attempts at winning a seat on the local school board, I decided to move out of Compton. My primary concern was the education of my children. The geographic change, however, had an unimaginable affect on my life and that of my family. The change in surroundings and the people with whom I interacted presented new opportunities for success.

Upon reflection:

My potential for success changes with every change in circumstances. If I feel thwarted in my abilities, I can change my surroundings. In doing so, I may unleash my potential. If I am not getting what I want out of life, I can move my living quarters. If I have a goal in mind but I cannot see a clear path to it, I can change my vantage point.

Circumstances are the who, what, when, and where of my actions and interactions. While the people and events of my surroundings may be beyond my control, I can alter my surroundings or the perception of the opportunities that the circumstances present.

I cannot stop or accelerate the movement of time, but I can change the actual or amount of time that I dedicate to an activity.

I may not be able to change the attitudes of the people with whom I deal, but I can deal with other people.

I can move my geographic location and I can change how material things affect my living.

I ought not leave my life and success to chance. Instead, I should seek to maximize my control over circumstances to make them favorable to my purpose. There are several ways for me to maximize control. I can discover my habits and break the routine. I can visit a place where I have not yet been. I can join a new organization. I can take a class on a subject on which I know nothing. The exposure to new things, different places, or unfamiliar subjects will expand my horizons and increase my control over circumstances.

****

Reflect also on: ADVERSITY, CHANGE, OPPORTUNITY.

OPPORTUNITY

Seize the opportunity; do not wait for it to knock.

For the break after my first year of law school, I sought summer employment as did most of my classmates. I checked out the announcements of employment opportunities posted on the bulletin boards. Nothing appeared to be suited for me. I sought counsel from my faculty advisor.

The advisor and I spent a few moments discussing the type of work first-year law students did in the summer. All involved research, which I would not be able to do without the law firm hiring another person as a reader. Then we began creating jobs that would fit my abilities and meet the needs of employers. We came up with a job involving the initial screening of calls to determine the nature of the law involved so that the call could be properly routed in an office of hundreds of lawyers. The advisor had a friend who needed such a service. Thus, I found part-time work which I did during all breaks while in law school.

Upon reflection:

I need not wait for opportunity to knock. If I learn to recognize it, I can seize it.

Opportunity is not a matter of luck. It is not a question of being in the right place at the right time. That is only true if I am one that sits and waits for opportunity to come my way. If indeed it knocks just once, much of my life would be spent wondering if I missed the call. Or thinking that I missed my golden chance, I would waste precious time and energy bemoaning the fact that I missed my one opportunity.

Opportunity is a combination of circumstances that is favorable to my purpose. To recognize it, I must be fully aware of my purpose, of my goals, and of my objectives.

When I am presented with a set of circumstances, I should not label it as good or bad, positive or negative, or beneficial or adverse. Instead, I should simply study carefully the situation to find how it can be used to achieve my purpose.

Perhaps the circumstances suggest that I modify my goals and objectives. An event that sets me back may be a mere adjustment in my schedule so that the ultimate timing of completion is right. Maybe the situation is the necessary forerunner of what is vital to my ultimate success. In short, every day and each event of my life is the right time and an opportunity for me to move in the direction of my goals. When I accept that, nothing that I face will stop me from getting what I want or from being who I want to be.

It is not always clear that what happens to me is purposeful. But if I am confident about my destination and the path that I have chosen, I can accept by faith that God will direct me without error.

****

Reflect also on: ADVERSITY, CHALLENGE, CIRCUMSTANCES, PURPOSE.

OPTIONS

If you plan with multiple alternatives, you can avoid the option of quitting.

A member of my senior class asked me what I planned to do after graduating from Yale. I responded that I hoped to go to law school. He was astounded that I had only applied to four schools. He had applied to fifteen law schools and had already been rejected by four. I told him that if I did not get accepted at one of the four schools--Yale, Stanford, University of California at Berkeley, and University of Southern California, I would find something else to do. I was accepted by the latter two.

Upon reflection:

One sure way to achieve success in this life is to plan for it. Of course, my plans look to the future without my knowing what lies ahead. My plans must be flexible enough to deal with the unexpected barriers that I may confront. To obtain this needed flexibility I must always keep my options open. Having multiple options allows me to maintain control instead of being subject to circumstances.

While I must have an ultimate destination toward which I will move, I should keep in mind the alternatives that will also fulfill my dreams. I need not plan to spend the rest of my life doing one thing or another. There is nothing wrong with having one profession for a period of time and changing to another. Most often we choose what we want to do in life when we are young and lack the knowledge of all of the possibilities. I do not have to stick with my first choice.

At each critical point in my plans, I should provide multiple paths to take. For example, in charting my course of education, I considered several colleges instead of applying to only one. If I had done the latter, I would have had to scrap my plans had I not been accepted. When considering employment, as another example, I should not limit myself to one geographic location. I can always identify my first choice but have more than one choice.

My plans can be flexible with regard to my time line for reaching my goal. I must be prepared for that incident that would dictate that I delay my pursuits for a year or two or ten. While I am not promised longevity, I will plan for it and not let delays in reaching my goals stop me altogether.

****

Reflect also on: GOALS, OBSTACLES.

CHANGE

Fight change and you will often find yourself against the ropes.

Twenty-two years ago, I was a college undergraduate; now I am an administrative law judge. I was single; now I am married with four children. My income is twenty-eight times what it was two decades ago. Few of the friends with whom I associated in the early seventies do I associate with today. My life has significantly changed with the passage of time. I did not always notice the change, but a retrospective look shows it clearly. The change has been for the better.

Upon reflection:

As the seconds tick away, my life is changing. The change is so gradual that I do not recognize it. But when I look over the past year, five years, the last decade, or the past two decades of my life, I notice the difference. If I am yet moving on my path of success and continue to enjoy life, the change is for the better.

Each new moment brings with it a new set of circumstances. In each new set is another chance to move closer to my goals. Each day I will look for the new opportunity and continue to move forward.

If I recognize change and resist it, I will become a casualty of it. The force of change will eventually run me down when I bristle up and try to stop it. I cannot stop time, so I cannot stop the change that it carries. Instead of resisting, I should determine its direction and harness its power for my benefit.

Sometimes change is sudden. If I face change that is sudden and dramatic, I must not fear or fight it. Rather, I can permit it to push me out of my sphere of comfort. I can allow it to snatch from me my security blanket. The exposure to new conditions can help to reaffirm my resolve to obtain the most out of life and it can strengthen my will to succeed.

Change is inevitable, so I should plan for it. I can establish my course to success in a way that includes several options that I can readily take when there is a change in circumstances. I can be prepared mentally for change--that is, I can keep my imagination roaming the field of possibilities.

****

Reflect also on: ADAPTABILITY, CIRCUMSTANCES.

OBSTACLES

If you look for obstacles, you will find them.

I responded to the announcement of the opportunity to spend my junior year studying in Cairo, Egypt, by filing my application. The dean of students seemed to be supportive but telephoned me to say that I would not be granted an interview. The representative from the American University of Cairo believed that the lack of paved roads and the absence of signal lights would be barriers to my getting around the Egyptian capital. No arguments of mine could persuade her, and I was not interviewed. Her attitude was a greater obstacle than the unpaved streets and unregulated intersections.

Upon reflection:

The greatest obstacle that could get in the way of my achieving the success and joy of life is my attitude. If I lack an attitude of joy, I will feel sorrow with every disappointment. If I do not possess an attitude of success, I will see failure in every deterrent. The disappointments and deterrents will then appear to be greater barriers than they really are because of my attitude toward them.

The negativism of family or friends can also be a major obstacle between me and my goals. Because my mind is open to the advice of the people I love, their statements such as "It can't be done" or "It will never work" could find acceptance in my mental makeup. If that were to happen, they would become challenges for me to overcome. The strength of my will can hurdle me over such negativism.

When I have removed my obstructive attitude and hurdled the negativism of others, I will see a clear path around the actual obstacle that I face. My firm resolve will lead me to the alternate route to bypass the unexpected detour. The fervor of my desire will kindle the creativity to find another vehicle for getting me where I want to go.

The promise of abundance does not include a guarantee that my road to success will be smooth. I should be prepared for the stop-and-go and the detours. If I relax and take my time, I will eventually get there.

****

Reflect also on: ATTITUDE, NEGATIVISM.

CHALLENGE

If today you are not challenged, you will miss tomorrow's opportunity to improve yourself and your position in life.

I never once considered that I would not be able to complete my undergraduate studies at Yale within four years. The challenge was to complete my studies without the support system that I had in high school.

When I made the decision to attend Yale, I knew that the college textbooks would not be in braille. I would have to rely on tape recordings and would have to obtain them on my own because there would be no resource teacher. What's more, I chose to attend school three thousand miles away from home--away from the friends and family on whom I could rely for reading assistance and emotional support. I met the challenge and graduated with my class.

Upon reflection:

I have yet to meet a person who has not faced a challenge of one sort or another. Inevitably, each of us will find him- or herself in a situation that calls for a stronger effort, that demands creativity in approach, and/or that tests the strength of one's will. Since we all face them at one time or another, the question is not the challenge but rather the response.

When I am in a difficult spot, I should allow myself to bemoan the unfortunate situation. Balance of body, mind, and soul requires the emotional release. But I must not wallow in self-pity. I must remember the objective of my efforts and the success for which I strive. Then I can analyze the challenge with which I am confronted to find in it the opportunity that will move me forward once again.

I can talk to someone about the problem to help relieve my frustration and to readjust my focus from the challenge to the opportunity. However, I should share my concerns only with those who will encourage me to move on and not with one who will eagerly invite me into his or her company of commiseration.

I do not always have control over the events that occur in my life, but I can control my responses to them. I can ensure that the challenging circumstances are temporary. Even when I have a permanent condition such as the loss of sight, my adaptation to that condition makes it no longer a challenge.

****

Reflect also on: ADAPTABILITY, OBSTACLES, OPPORTUNITY.

OPTIMISM

Even a pessimist is optimistic about his ability to see the dark side of any circumstance.

Because the neighborhood kids did not want me to join in their games, often I played ball alone. One of my solitary games entailed throwing a rubber ball on the slanted roof of the house and waiting for it to roll down. The object was to catch it before it hit the ground. I could hear the ball as it rolled down the roof. Using a bright red ball (I could see colors until I was sixteen), I had fun playing the game. Occasionally I would lose the ball when I missed it and it stopped rolling on the ground. As I walked around the yard looking for a red object, everything I saw appeared to be red. Invariably I would kick the ball before I actually saw it.

Upon reflection:

Whatever I focus on, that is what I will see. If I set my focus of life to be optimism, I will see the optimum that can be obtained in life and its component experiences.

If I want success, I must look for it in every endeavor. If I want joy, I must feel it in all that I do. If I want to live life to the fullest, I must know when the cup is full. My view of success, my feeling of joy, and my knowledge of the best can only come through optimism.

To be optimistic is not to live in a fantasy of utopia. Optimism permits me to look at an imperfect situation and make the best of it. Faced with difficulties or faced with adversities, I see life as working to fullness and not toward diminution.

Optimism is a belief that will permeate, illuminate, and stimulate my mind. It is the ray of hope that pierces through clouds of despair. It is the elucidation of purpose when my efforts seem to be pointless. It is the fervor of determination when quitting would be the easy way out. Moreover, optimism radiates beyond me to reveal the best that is in others.

****

Reflect also on: ATTITUDE, BELIEFS, FOCUS.

ADAPTABILITY

The fullness of life can be enjoyed only by those who have the ability to adapt to the continual change in circumstances.

I can readily identify two times in my life when the ability to adapt was key to the avoidance of stress and to the continued enjoyment of life. The first occurred when I was four years old. Adjusting to life as a blind individual in a sighted world was easy. At age four, not only did I know little about the role that sight would play in life, but making change was less stressful.

The second test of adaptability came when I was thirty. Without a doubt, adapting to married life was the more severe test. Giving up thirty years of behavior as a single man was not easy even though it was my desire to do so. In fact, after thirteen years of marriage, there are yet changes to which I must be able to adapt. Without the ability to make the necessary adjustments in our relationship, Jaci and I could not continue to enjoy life together.

Upon reflection:

Adaptability is key to living and enjoying life in abundance. My life is a chain of events, no two of which are identical. Each day that I live is different and my ability to adapt to change determines how well I will fare.

When life serves me a bowl of cherries, I must learn to either remove the pits or eat around them.

I cannot ignore their existence but must adapt in order to deal with the annoyance.

When life presents me with shattered dreams, I must learn to string the broken pieces together to make a wind chime. If the wind blows too hard for my chime, I can build a windmill and generate for myself power. Realizing dreams is realizing endless possibilities. To take advantage of the other possibilities may require adaptation.

When life hands me a rose, I will not complain about the thorns. I will appreciate the beauty of the flower--its color and fragrance--and search out the bush from which it came. I am sure to find more. I must learn to cultivate the source of opportunity to reap continual benefits.

It does not matter where I am today. I can be sure that tomorrow will present a different set of circumstances. My ability to adapt to the change will determine my success.

****

Reflect also on: CHANGE, CIRCUMSTANCES, OPTIMISM.

ADVERSITY

Whether or not the condition, situation, or set of circumstances with which you are faced is an adversity depends on how you look at it.

Many, perhaps even most, people would consider it to be an adversity to be unable to see. I do not. During the forty years that I have been blind, only once did I wish that I could see. That one wish came in the midst of self-pity.

Being blind did not stop me from obtaining a bachelor's degree in mathematics from Yale or from getting my law degree from the University of Southern California. The greater challenge was not the blindness but the convincing of the schools' admissions committees that I could complete the courses of study despite my blindness.

Being blind does not stop me from making pizza or from mowing my lawn. By substituting imagination and creativity for sight, I can use my sense of touch as well as my other senses to get the job done.

Upon reflection:

What is an adversity anyway? It is a condition, situation, or set of circumstances that is unfavorable to my purpose or objectives. While my blindness is a permanent condition and my ethnicity and gender are characteristics which I cannot change, they are adversities only if I allow them to be.

I should often take a new look at myself and

my situation. When doing so, I must be careful not to apply the label "adversity" to the circumstances or conditions that are different from the "norm" or from what I desire them to be. When I use that label, I give myself license to quit. I find in it the excuse for not trying, for not trying again, or for not trying a different approach. I must remember that an adversity is something unfavorable to my purpose or goals. So the condition or situation is not adverse if I can find in it something favorable. It will then become an opportunity.

Though the situation may appear to be unfavorable to my purpose, it need not cause me to miss my fortune. I can respond to a sudden or unexpected event by reviewing my goals to ensure that any setback is only temporary. A loss of a job, a rejected application, and a relationship that is ended are events that are transitory unless I choose to make them permanent obstacles to my joy and success by waddling in self-pity.

If I experience a permanent change of circumstances, a change over which I have no control, I need not abandon my quest but rather modify the approach to my goal. By using imagination and creativity, I can find the way to use to my advantage the new course that I am forced to take.

****

Reflect also on: CHALLENGE, CIRCUMSTANCES, OPPORTUNITY, PURPOSE.

TEMPERANCE

Temperance is the state of control where the joy and fullness of life is attained through moderation and balance.

My wife and I make at least an annual trip to Las Vegas. I have an affinity for visiting the city because there is where we had our first date--a weekend date shortly after she moved to California.

My game of choice is keno. I have a fascination with numbers. Though I cannot see the screen showing the keno board, a ten by eight array of the numbers from 1 to 80, I can randomly choose a set of numbers to play by touching the screen with the pointer. As each number is selected, the machine emits a tone. Thus, I can count how many numbers I have played.

In each game, the machine will draw twenty of the eighty numbers. A player can attempt to match up to ten. I am rather successful at hitting three of three (for $11.50 on a quarter bet).

When the game is played, the machine beeps for each of the twenty numbers drawn. The pitch of the beep is higher when one of my chosen numbers is matched. I can count the higher-pitched beeps to determine how many of my numbers are drawn, though I do not know which they are unless someone reads the game results to me.

Recently I played keno in the Mirage Resort of Las Vegas. Sitting at a machine next to the white tigers, I was able to play for four hours, taking only ten dollars from my pocket. I walked away with a modest gain of fifty dollars. Yes, I was happy. I do not go to Las Vegas to get rich but to have fun. I take with me a fixed amount of money to play. Otherwise, I could be induced by the pleasure of it to play to excess.

Upon reflection:

I have been admonished from time to time to drink or to eat in moderation. I know well that excessive drinking or eating is harmful to my body. The same is true for any activity in which I engage. Too much of it is not good for me. I should strive to be temperate in all matters.

Temperance is the result of taking control of my life--body, mind, and soul. It is knowing when to say "no" and when to say "yes". Such knowledge comes from understanding how I am affected by my activities and outside stimuli. Temperance is the ability to choose the results that are best for me and to avoid being enslaved by my desires.

Self-control can be developed, but placing myself in the path of temptation is not the way to strengthen my grip. I can achieve moderation by creating the circumstances that will permit moderation. I should limit the amount of food that I have in my reach if eating is my excess. I can stay away from the people who rile me up when I am subject to uncontrollable anger. When I can identify my area of weakness and can create the temperate circumstances, I am exercising control.

****

Reflect also on: BALANCE, CONTROL.

14

STUMBLING BLOCKS

I need not treat rejection as an indication that I am not qualified. Instead, it can be the impetus for my determination or the catalyst of a revised approach.

In life as in arithmetic, no matter how small the amount, a negative factor will render a negative product.

DEPENDENCE

Self-confidence can be built on support but is undermined by dependence.

Without hesitation, I dismissed Byron's suggestion that I organize a church. Byron was one of a small group of people who joined Jaci and me for Bible discussions. We all were disillusioned with traditional Christian Sunday services.

This group gathering for purpose of fellowship and Bible study was the second of which my wife and I had been a part. Before moving to Lancaster, we had Bible discussions with a few other couples, rotating from home to home with the host and hostess being the discussion leaders.

I rejected Byron's idea of establishing a church because I do not want a congregation to develop a dependent relationship with me as their intermediary to God. For the very same reason I had, ten years prior, rejected an offer to pastor a small congregation.

Upon reflection:

If my life is to have meaning, it must be shared. Hence, I enhance life the more that I interact with others. But I devitalize myself and diminish my self-esteem with dependence.

I ought not think of dependence only in context of drugs and alcohol. Because of their destruction of the body and alteration of the mind, they interfere with the enjoyment of the fullness of life. They provide only an illusion of happiness and/or temporary release from life's struggles.

I must be cognizant of dependence in all its forms. I should avoid the mental dependence that was created in my educational upbringing. I do not need a teacher or instructor to impart knowledge to me. I can learn on my own and think for myself. If I am mentally independent, I do not have to accept the negative or limiting beliefs of someone else.

I must avoid the spiritual dependence which can come through religious devotion. I can, and must, have direct contact with God in order to realize the maximum of my spiritual potential. I must keep myself free of the one who would lead me to believe that only through him or her can I interact with the Supreme Spirit of the universe. The one who so teaches obviously does not understand the omnipresence of God.

Not only should I avoid being physically, mentally, and spiritually dependent on another, but I must conduct myself in such a way that no one becomes dependent on me. I must ensure that my wife maintains her independence even though we are committed to each other. I must teach my children independence by teaching them to think, to reason, to feel, and to be responsible for their own actions. When others look to me for advice or guidance, I should share experiences and knowledge while allowing them to make the decisions.

****

Reflect also on: CONFORMITY, HELP, INDEPENDENCE.

REJECTION

If you shield yourself from rejection, you will eliminate the possibility of your acceptance.

Clarissa was a second-year student in the Graduate School of Music when I was a junior at Yale. My love for her helped me to ignore the fact that I was a few years younger and that she might not, because of the age difference, have a romantic interest in me. We frequently saw each other in Berkeley, one of Yale's twelve residential colleges, where we both had meal contracts. To watch television was my convenient excuse for visiting her in her dormitory room.

Because of my insecurities in romantic relationships occasioned by my blindness, I timidly pursued my interest in Clarissa. I ended my pursuit altogether when I learned of the other guys who were interested in her. They were a freshman, a senior, and a second-year graduate student. They all had sight. Fearing that I would be rejected because of my blindness, I stopped visiting Clarissa and tried to avoid meeting her in the dining hall. I bought a television to watch in my own room and there I secluded myself. I discovered later--when it was too late--that I was the one in whom she was interested.

Upon reflection:

The possibility of being rejected is a risk that I must be willing to take. Otherwise, I will miss opportunities that may not be presented again. The college that I wanted to attend could not admit an unlimited number of applicants; some had to be rejected. The position that I desire cannot be offered to every interviewee; all but one must be rejected. The contract for which I bid can only be awarded to one; the other bidders will be rejected. The possibility of being rejected is ever present. That chance of rejection ought not hinder my applying for the position or bidding for the work.

I must not view rejection as a manifestation of a lack of worth. Instead, I can see it as the rejecter's inability to appreciate the value that I can add.

I need not treat rejection as an indication that I am not qualified. Instead, it can be the impetus for my determination or the catalyst of a revised approach.

There is also the possibility that the rejection will work to my advantage. There may be coming soon another opportunity that I would have to pass if not rejected from my present bid.

I can overcome a fear of rejection by enhancing my self-esteem. When I am highly confident of my potential to get the most out of life, I will not be shaken by a "no". With a high self-esteem, my purpose in life remains in focus, and I will see another way to obtain joy and satisfaction.

****

Reflect also on: FEAR, SELF-ESTEEM.

UNCERTAINTY

If you wish to avoid the uncertain, do nothing and you will be certain to get nothing.

In Atlanta, Georgia, at the 1991 convention of Toastmasters International, I placed second in the World Championship of Public Speaking. Initially, I was pleased with my achievement and did not plan to compete again. After all, my goal had been to compete in, as opposed to winning, the championship contest. One matter that concerned me was the possibility of doing worse than second. Perhaps not even making it to the final event. The uncertainty of what would result in the next year, however, did not stop me. The absolute certainty was that if I did not compete, I could not win.

Upon reflection:

There is no endeavor that I can undertake of which I can be absolutely certain of its outcome. I have no idea when my time will run out, so every time I act I do so with uncertainty. I assume that I will see tomorrow. I must interact with persons over whom I have no control. Building relationships on trust, I continue to interact with them. Everything in life is done in the midst of uncertainty.

There exists a level of uncertainty or risk above which I will not act. That level of uncertainty is my "ceiling of risk". If I have a low ceiling of risk, I will act only when I can reasonably predict the outcome. If my ceiling is high, I am willing to take a chance in the midst of low probability.

If I can function with a high ceiling of risk, I can set for myself loftier goals, and I will have more room within which to operate in pursuit of those goals. On the other hand, the lower my ceiling of risk, the more restricted will be the things that I attain.

I can raise my ceiling of risk by being certain of what it is that I want; building my confidence in my ability to get what I want; and developing the self-assurance that because I am in control of my life, I will be able to handle and adjust to whatever the outcome chances to be.

****

Reflect also on: DOUBT.

FAILURE

Failure is not the lack of success but rather the lack of effort.

For my mathematics major I enrolled in a course on abstract algebra. What is abstract algebra? I do not know. It was apparently too abstract for me. I never understood the class lectures. The professor was the author of the text, and his explanations found in the unpublished manuscript were as clear as those presented in class. I sought assistance from Sue, who volunteered to record the text for me, but she too was unable to understand the subject. Neither of us received a passing grade. Nevertheless, I have a degree in mathematics.

Upon reflection:

I am not a failure. There have been times when I fell short of my goal, but those incidents do not make me a failure. From my experiences I gained knowledge and I moved closer to my objectives. Hence, I have achieved something.

I am not a failure. In the judgment of another I may not have made the mark, but what someone else thinks of me does not make me a failure. I will never measure my success by standards set by someone else.

The concept of failing was first implanted in my mind when I was in school. To successfully mold me into conformity, it was necessary for the educational institution to set up a mechanism to keep me in check. The fear of getting an "F" was that mechanism. Since society continues to grade my performance, I sometimes am faced with the fear of failing.

Though I am not a failure, I set myself up to fail by living to please someone else instead of pursuing the desires of my heart. I set myself up to fail if I permit fear to stop me from taking the action that leads to what I want. I set myself up to fail when I disbelieve my ability to succeed.

Whenever I begin an endeavor, there is the chance that I will fall short of the desired mark. I must be willing to take that chance and make an attempt. Whatever I gain through my efforts is success. If I fall short of the goal, I can reset the mark, revise my approach, and try again. I have failed only when I refuse to try. By this restrictive definition of failure, I increase the probability of my success.

****

Reflect also on: ACHIEVEMENTS, CONFORMITY, FEAR, SUCCEED, SUCCESS.

DOUBT

If you see a shadow of doubt, look for hope in the light by which it is cast.

In my third year of law school, I started thinking about employment as an attorney. I applied only to government agencies. I did not bother to submit resumes to private firms because I doubted that they would hire me.

My doubtful attitude about private employment was based on a conversation I had with a blind instructor at Stanford University's law school. He told me that even though he finished in the top ten percent of his class, no private firm to which he applied offered him a job, but every government agency to which he submitted his resume did. Because my grades were not as good as his, I considered it a waste of time to seek employment with a private firm.

Upon reflection:

When it comes to enhancing my self-image, achieving success, and realizing my dreams, no doubt is reasonable. Doubt as small as a grain of mustard seed will negate faith of that same measure. Doubt is conceived in the absence of evidence that what I desire will come about. It is in that same absence of evidence that faith is activated. The two are mutually exclusive, and I alone can decide what will fill the void.

While doubt's primary victim is faith, it will

also assault my motivation and rob me of reasons to move forward.

Doubt dwells in the separation between what I want and what convention and reason say that I can get. The greater the separation, the more uncertain I am about my success. There are three approaches to this chasm. They are not mutually exclusive and may be used in combination.

I can fill the separation with faith. In other words, I can believe that it is possible even though I have no evidence that it has occurred or can happen.

I can bridge the gap with the support and encouragement of others. Their confidence in me can carry me through times of uncertainty.

I can close the gap with risk-taking effort. My successes will let me know that my desires are reasonable and attainable.

If I can just imagine the possibilities, I can begin the necessary steps to eliminating doubt.

****

Reflect also on: FAITH, UNCERTAINTY.

NEGATIVISM

In life as in arithmetic, no matter how small the amount, a negative factor will render a negative product.

I received a "B" as the final grade in my high school American Literature class. I asked the teacher why I received the low grade after she had indicated at mid term that I would probably receive an "A". She responded, "Because you have no writing style and your vocabulary is morose."

From that point until my first year at Yale I was insecure about my ability to write. My confidence in writing was turned around by my freshman-year English instructor, who wrote this comment on my first assignment: "I do not agree with what you say, but I love your writing style."

Upon reflection:

It is unfortunate, but there is a great deal of negativism in the world. As long as I am in the world, I will be exposed to it. Negative words alone can inflict severe injury. The harm can be immediate, but more often the negativism will incubate and, like a virus, infect my mind and attitude.

The first step to treating negative-itis is to purge my language of negativism. When referring to myself and my abilities, I should avoid the word "not" and its contraction "n't". I should eliminate the negative prefixes such as "im" of impossible, "un" of unqualified, and "in" of incompetent. When talking about others, not only must I avoid the words but also the negative tone or attitude.

Next I should quarantine myself to avoid contact with chronically negative people. I have to close my ears to their conversation. I ought to let them know that I do not wish to be infected with their gloom. This quarantine includes isolation from books, songs, movies, and other forms of entertainment which depict and promote negative behavior and negative attitudes. If I delight myself in what is negative, it will be difficult to treat the negative-itis.

Finally, as an antidote to negativism, I must inject my thoughts with positivism. For every negative thing said about me or my abilities, I will identify two positive ones. If I can double the positive for each negative, I will always remain in positiveness.

****

Reflect also on: ASSOCIATION.

CONFORMITY

The power that emanates from the soul is restrained by conformity to that which limits imagination, creativity, and expression.

It seemed, at the time of making such decisions, that most of the members of my graduating class were deciding to go either to law or medical school. Law over medicine appeared to be the practical choice for a blind man. In the midst of making plans for what I would do after leaving Yale, I received a telephone call from Harvey. He was in his first year of law school and wanted to encourage me to pursue law as a career.

Encouragement from Harvey was a primary force behind my decision to attend Yale. I found it to be a good choice. So when he suggested that I should go to law school, I accepted the idea. In summing up his first year, Harvey observed that law was a potent tool or weapon; law school was the attempt to teach you to use it in the way they believe it ought to be used. Harvey alluded to the thrill in learning the weapon but warned against conformity.

Upon reflection:

I have within me great power. I have the power to succeed, the capacity for excellence, and the choice to be joyful. The full impact of my potential is thwarted by conformity.

Conformity started when I was an infant. I was molded to conform by being taught that this color is not worn with that; girls do not play this way; boys do not play that way. Such teaching led me to place emphasis on physical characteristics and outward appearances.

Then I was sent to school where I was fed facts and figures and induced by a grade to regurgitate them on cue. Even in my art class, my natural tendency for creativity was brought into conformity with a grading of my ability to color within the lines.

At church, instead of teaching me how my faith could ignite the power within, I was issued a list of dos and don'ts--mostly the latter--in an effort to judge whether or not I conform to the established doctrines. I was frightened into believing that if I did not find God in their way, I would suffer eternal damnation.

My potential is imprisoned in conformity, with the fear of rejection being the jailer. I don my prison garb when I "dress for success". By "climbing the corporate ladder" I struggle to get out on good behavior.

There are necessary rules of conduct to govern a civilized society. By observing such rules and by conforming to my values and moral standards, I protect myself and the lives of others. But conformity which restrains thought, feelings, imagination, creativity, and expression tends to limit rather than enhance life.

****

Reflect also on: EMPOWERMENT, FEAR, RELIGION.

EXCUSES

The obstacles to success are best overcome by making adjustments instead of excuses.

Where many might have expected it, I did not use my blindness as an excuse. However, there were times when I made excuses for not completing a specific assignment.

For example, in high school, where most of my books were in braille, I used the fact that my fingers were cold as an excuse for not completing a reading assignment. Cold fingers are too numb to discern the various dot formations.

In law school, I got out of participating in the professors' Socratic lectures when I advised that the tape recordings of the texts had not yet been completed. I did not lie. But if I had wanted to complete the assignments, I could have gotten around the problems.

Upon reflection:

There are plenty of excuses that can be made. At one time or another everyone has found himself or herself in a position of disadvantage. And the excuses begin: I am an African-American in a society dominated by Whites. I am White and the law gives preference to ethnic minorities. I am a woman. I am too old. I am not old enough. I lack the necessary education. I have a physical impairment. It is not my job. I do not have the authority.

Whatever the circumstance, to use it as an

excuse can deprive one of joy and success.

When I make excuses, I permit myself to accept mediocrity instead of pursuing excellence. I give myself license to quit in the place of finding a way around the obstruction. I relinquish authority to determine my destiny and succumb to adverse circumstances. What then follows my excuses is my moaning and complaining about how unfair life is to me.

My readiness to make excuses is an indication of the weakness of my desire and the feebleness of my commitment. If my passion for a thing is strong enough, I will make adjustments in my approach to my goals.

I will let yesterday be the last day for my making excuses. I need not like the circumstances in which I find myself, but I can accept their existence and plan my strategy for changing them. If they cannot be changed by me, I should find a way to use the situation to my advantage.

****

Reflect also on: ADVERSITY, CIRCUMSTANCES, CONTROL.

COMFORT

To remain comfortable with where you are and what you are doing will assuredly result in stagnation.

I was comfortable with making inspirational presentations. I began speaking to youth groups in churches when I was sixteen years old. Shortly after finishing law school, I started speaking to students at school career day events. So when Maurice asked me to speak at his wedding, I was undaunted. I thought that an inspirational presentation about the importance of communication to hold a marriage together would be perfect.

However, Maurice had something else in mind. He wanted me to give a humorous speech. He said, "I want the people laughing at my wedding. I want you to make the guests roll in the aisles."

I lost sleep trying to prepare a humorous speech. But on June 25, 1988, I fulfilled Maurice's request. I made the people laugh. Having to do the speech led to my joining Toastmasters International, competing in its World Championship of Public Speaking, and eventually pursuing professional speaking as a business.

Upon reflection:

Relief from day to day problems and toils is necessary. Rest, relaxation and recreation are important to my physical, mental, and spiritual health and well-being. I need to take time to find a comfortable place where I can restore the body, refresh the mind, and rejuvenate the soul. But I should not seek to be comfortable when I am at work, operating my business, or otherwise pursuing success.

When I am comfortable in my job or profession, I cannot realize my full potential. Comfort can be the bane of my creativity, innovation, and dreams. I will not be challenged if I am comfortable. I will not make an effort to change my surroundings when I am comfortable.

A sure sign that I am working in comfort is my functioning by rote or habit. When I operate in a rut, my body is active but my mind and soul are in a holding pattern. I am not mentally stimulated so I am not thinking or learning. I must be willing to break my routine in order to grow.

My limitations are defined by what I desire to do in light of my physical and mental capacities. To further develop my skills, I must be willing to extend myself to new limits. When I get comfortable with the new reaches, I must stretch a little further. I will never know the outer limits of my capacities unless I extend myself into new areas.

I must be willing to try something new. If I continue to do what I am currently doing, I will get the same results as I have gotten before. If I want something different, I must try doing it in a new way, at a different time, in another place, and/or with a different person.

****

Reflect also on: HABIT.

15

IMPETUS TO SUCCEED

Only I can establish what will serve as an incentive for me. As involuntary as breathing, I formulate a hierarchy of interests and desires.

Life's awards of love and joy and success are given to me each day that I contribute the most that I have to living.

INCENTIVES

If your desire is sufficiently strong, you need no incentive, just opportunity.

In high school I participated in the National Forensic League, winning gold medals in oratorical interpretation, poetry interpretation, and impromptu speaking. I loved the competition. Hence, there was no question in my mind that I would enter the speech contests sponsored by Toastmasters International. As soon as I learned about the contest, I made plans to enter. I needed no incentive to enter. The honor of being the World Champion of Public Speaking, however, was the incentive for my working harder to do my best.

Upon reflection:

There is a variety of things that will ignite my engine and put me into motion. Sometimes it is money or praise or rewards. At other times it is happiness or a hunger for knowledge or the satisfaction of helping another. This is not an exhaustive list, and the presence of one does not exclude another. Whatever it is, it is an incentive for me.

I am motivated--that is, my engine is ignited--when I have a compelling reason to act. Incentives are the compelling reasons. "Compelling" is a key element for an incentive to be effective. I may have the desire to acquire money, but $100 will not compel me to walk across hot coals. A bowl of soup and a sandwich might, on the other hand, stimulate a man who has not eaten in a week to do it.

Only I can establish what will serve as an incentive for me. As involuntary as breathing, I formulate a hierarchy of interests and desires. Even if I cannot verbalize the priority, my actions will reveal what is compelling to me.

Someone else may be able to induce me to change my priorities by offering a larger carrot. My interest in avoiding pain is greater than my desire for money when $100 does not impel me to do the hot-coals walk. However, if the payment is raised to one million dollars, I might be prompted to rearrange my priorities. When the change in reward induces me to rearrange my priorities, it becomes evident what is an incentive for me.

****

Reflect also on: INSPIRATION, MONEY, MOTIVATION.

MONEY

Money rules those who must pay for yesterday's pleasure but serves those who know the joy of tomorrow.

I was not at all surprised to learn that before I got married (at age thirty) my brothers and sisters often talked about why I had no money. They could not understand how I could be working full time, be single, have no children, and be paying low rent and still have no money. If they had only bothered to ask me, I could have told them.

Money means very little to me. Hence, it was not unusual for me to give it away, both to charitable organizations and to friends who were in need. In fact, my siblings were often the object of my giving.

Upon reflection:

How much of life am I willing to give up for money? What do I sacrifice while chasing that elusive dollar? I can learn the answers to these questions by making a list of what I would do and how I would spend my time if money were no object.

What would I do with my time if I did not have to work for a living? My time is my life. Considering the hours that I am awake, a significant part of life is spent on the job. If I dislike my job, I make life miserable for myself by going to it. If there are activities in which I would rather be involved but I forego them to go to work, I sacrifice life for the need to make money.

And for what would I use my income and

resources if not for my daily needs of food, clothing, shelter, transportation, and health? I have desire for things which cost money. Yet, I do not get what I want even though I work because my money is obligated to meet the necessities of life. But what is really necessary? I must be careful not to become a slave to the dollar for things that do not make me happy.

If I am not careful, I will sacrifice the fullness of life and forego joy for the almighty dollar. Not for the dollar itself but for the gratification obtained from spending it.

If I am not careful, I can fall into the trap of paying today for the gratification of yesterday. Gratification from material things is temporary at best and the pleasure of them will fade though the price is not quickly forgotten. The upward spiral will continue as I seek to amass enough money to pay for past pleasures and buy present happiness. In the endless chase there will be no joy for the future.

Once I am enticed by material things and/or am hooked by debt, money becomes the incentive for what I do.

****

Reflect also on: INCENTIVES, PURPOSE.

COMPETITION

The competitive edge is desire and ability sharpened with excellence and tenacity.

By the time I reached the regional level of the 1992 Toastmasters' international speech competition, I had participated in fourteen speech contests within twenty-eight months. Competing was exciting. I had succeeded in garnering the first-place trophy in all but two of the contests.

But for some reason I lacked the energy and enthusiasm for the 1992 regional competition. I did not feel like being there. Fortunately, I drew number 7 for the speaking order. I was able to hear six of my seven competitors before it was my turn to speak. With each succeeding speech, my energy level increased. By the time my name and speech title were announced, I was ready to give my all. I won the contest.

Upon reflection:

I ought not shy away from competition. It can be the inducement for me to put forth the extra effort that will get me over the top. There will be times when I do not feel like giving it my very best. I may not always be in top physical condition. Sometimes my mind will be distracted from the purpose of my endeavor. At times I may be emotionally drained from all in which I am involved. The need to maintain a competitive edge will, however, motivate me to work despite these adverse conditions.

To have the competitive edge requires focus. I must keep my eye on the goal and my mind on the reasons for pursuing that goal. My focus must be on the product of my effort not the prize. The competitive edge involves more than the desire to win the title of "Number One". It includes satisfaction of purpose.

I can retain the competitive edge by maintaining a standard of excellence. I ought not compete to outdo my opponent but rather to excel my own performance. I can outdo my competitor by destroying him or her while maintaining for myself a level of mediocrity. In the end, both of us are losers.

Competition can be fierce when there is but one position at the top and many vying for the prize. The fierceness should not be from the competitors destroying each other, but rather from each person doing his or her very best.

****

Reflect also on: DESIRE, EXCELLENCE, WINNING.

MOTIVATION

Motivation is the mind's ability to convince the body to act when inaction would be the desirable thing.

Throughout my years of schooling, I was self-motivated. Though I needed support from others in gaining admission to Yale and the University of Southern California, I needed little encouragement from others to complete my courses of study. The same was true for taking the bar examination and for seeking employment. However, after obtaining a decent and steady job, getting married, and having children, I got comfortable. I stopped setting for myself new goals. My wife Jacqueline helps me to avoid stagnation. She suggests new projects and encourages me to pursue new goals. It is through her inspiration and encouragement that I am motivated.

Upon reflection:

It is possible for me to know what I want and to set my goals yet fail to attain success because I lack motivation. To be motivated is to have a reason to act--a reason that is so compelling that it moves me forward. I am self-motivated when I alone identify those compelling reasons. I am self-motivated if I need no one else to remind me of those compelling reasons when disappointment or despair would otherwise thwart my efforts.

I was born with the capacity to motivate myself. However, that innate self-motivating ability is blunted by constant bombardment with negative words and disappointing events. Because my mind can become cluttered with deprecating thoughts, feelings of inadequacy, or recollections of failure, I need help at times to find the reasons for moving forward. To keep my motivating abilities in tune, I must seek out sources of positive reinforcement. From a book, a sermon, or a friend's encouragement I can regain vitality and enthusiasm to act in my own interest.

Motivation must come from within. My wife, a friend, or a motivational speaker might suggest to me reasons for moving forward, but for those reasons to be compelling, I must adopt them as my own.

To maintain my forward motion, I must devise a way to keep fresh in my mind the reasons for acting. I have to focus on the objectives not the obstacles. I must recount my achievements not my failures. When I share with another, I have to emphasize the positive not the negative.

****

Reflect also on: INCENTIVES, INSPIRATION, PASSIONATE.

INSPIRATION

Inspiration is the soul's breath of creativity, innovation, and development.

The moment was electrifying as the president announced the winner of the 1991 speech contest for Region 2 of Toastmasters International. I was excited to hear my name, knowing that the next step would be the World Championship of Public Speaking.

I could not see the crowd standing before me but I sensed their presence as they waited in line to offer congratulations. In the midst of the handshakes, one lady grasped my right hand and continued to shake it as she suggested, "People pay hundreds of dollars to hear someone like you speak."

Never before had I considered the idea of professional speaking. I was already motivated to speak; she inspired me to do it as a business.

Upon reflection:

I am inspired when a spoken word, an event, or some other outside stimulus or force prompts emotion or infuses new ideas or concepts into my mind. The thoughts need not be new to the universe. If they are new to me, it is inspiration.

Inspiration can be motivational. When I am instilled with new ideas or creative concepts, I may be given new compelling reasons to move forward. I am motivated to complete the article, write the poem, record the speech, or develop the product.

I cannot be inspired and motivated unless my mind is receptive and open to new ideas. I must be receptive to the source of new possibilities. For example, God cannot be a source of inspiration to me if I do not acknowledge God's existence. I must also be receptive to the concept. I cannot be inspired to develop a new product if I do not believe that there is a way to improve upon the old.

I should seek to be inspired. For it, I have to keep my mind open to feeling and creativity--to new ideas and concepts. I should find a place and time of quietude where and when I can allow my thoughts to flow without interruption.

****

Reflect also on: INCENTIVES, MOTIVATION.

ACHIEVEMENTS

Whatever they are and whenever they occur, your achievements are great and should be applauded.

"What do you consider to be your greatest achievement?" Jaci asked me as we relaxed in New Orleans following a speaking engagement.

I had to think a moment before answering. I considered some of the things that I had succeeded in doing and found them all to be applaudable. Graduating from Yale University with a bachelor's degree in mathematics. Obtaining a law degree from the University of Southern California. Passing the California Bar. Marrying Jaci. Having my four children. Winning Toastmasters International's World Championship of Public Speaking.

After some time thinking about her question, I had no real answer for Jaci as to which is the greatest. Each is significant in a way that makes comparisons impossible. Each makes my life rich. In the absence of either, things would be very different for me today.

Upon reflection:

I need not concern myself with labelling one or the other of my accomplishments as the greatest. So long as I am moving in the direction of my goals, the last step that I took is the greatest, but the next one will be even greater.

What is important is that I remember to take a moment to remind myself of what I have achieved.

Each step that I take that advances me toward my goal is worth noting and applauding. As often as I need to I will celebrate my successes.

When I lack confidence in my ability to attain my ultimate goal, I can regain my self-assurance by looking back at what I have already done.

When repeated negative assaults on me cause me to lose self-esteem, I can find again respect in my abilities by reminding myself how I overcame previous challenges.

Every time I reach a milestone, I should celebrate. What constitutes a milestone depends on the challenges that had to be overcome in order to reach the goal. When an infant utters "mama" for the first time, it is applauded. But not so when the child is able to form complete sentences. For a user of a wheelchair to participate in the marathon is more of an event for him or her to celebrate than for one who has no restriction of mobility.

As I celebrate my successes, I must remember to be humble. My achievements do not make me superior over another person who has not yet accomplished what I have. Nor will my achievements exempt me from failure tomorrow.

****

Reflect also on: BEGINNINGS, ENCOURAGEMENT, GOALS.

WINNING

You will always win when you give your best, so long as first is not your quest.

Jaci and I helped our son Dana form his entry into the Pinewood Derby sponsored by Boys Scouts. I showed him how to use the hand saw, wood files, and planer to get the shape that he wanted. Jaci assisted with painting. After nailing on the wheels, applying the graphite, and inserting the weights, the car was ready. I rolled it in the palm of my hand and noted that the wheels were not aligned. There was no time to make the needed adjustments. So, as I handed the car to him, I suggested to Dana that it probably would not win a race, but it would roll.

Dana, who was eight years old at the time, responded, "I am not concerned with winning. I just want to be in the race."

Dana did, in fact, win the first-place trophy.

Upon reflection:

In the game of life what does it mean to win? Does the first-place prize go to the person who lives the longest? Does it go to the individual who amasses the most wealth? Does it go to the person who achieves the greatest fame? It is neither fame, wealth, nor longevity that determines the winner. Winning is simply entering the race to give it my best effort.

I can win only if I know with clarity what it is that I want from life. Knowing the ultimate prize determines the effort that I will put forth to win. It is then that I can assess my talents and abilities and know how to apply them to get what I want. Winning is knowing the game and playing it with all that I have.

Winning in life is not simply a matter of who comes in first, and I need not wait until the race is over to get my trophy. Life's awards of love and joy and success are given to me each day that I contribute the most that I have to living. I am winning when I am giving my best and getting the most for my efforts.

I have been endowed with the necessary talents to win. The opportunity is there. The starting shot has been fired, but it is not too late to get into the race. We do not all start at the same time and the finish line is drawn in a different place for each of us. I just need to get into the race and give it my best. Only then will I win. If I cross the finish line having lived in mediocrity, I lose.

****

Reflect also on: ABILITY, COMPETITION, EXCELLENCE, TALENT.

SPIRITUALITY

It is through faith, not by sight or logic, that you see your spiritual connection to your surroundings.

I was once religious. I went to church every time there were services--Sunday morning, Sunday night, Tuesday night, Friday night. I attended choir rehearsals when I was not in the choir. I worked at the church on Saturdays. I followed the routines and rituals of the church without understanding their significance.

Today, I attempt to pattern my life after the teachings of Christ but am reluctant to call myself a Christian. That label is used by so many, and I do not agree with the doctrine of many others who claim the identity. I choose, instead, to describe myself as spiritual.

Upon reflection:

There are those who call it Christianity while others call it Buddhism. It can be labeled religion or atheism. One can live by the doctrines of Judaism, Islam, Hinduism, or whatever sect one chooses. Each is an expression of spiritual choice.

Regarding my spiritual connection to the universe, I have three options available to me.

First, I can disbelieve that I have a soul or deny that my soul has a connection with the eternal universe. To exercise this option is to limit my life to the finiteness of my body. Though my mind, through imagination and dreams, can escape the bounds of time and space, I will act only on those things which I can logically connect with physical reality.

Second, I can believe in the existence of my soul being and recognize its eternal and universal characteristics. Such belief includes the knowledge of an eternal and universal spiritual being, which I might call God, Higher Power, Force of Nature, etc. However, my connection with this eternal and universal spiritual being comes only after the death of my body. While I recognize the existence of a supernatural being, my mind operates within the finiteness of the body. I will call on the supernatural only when I reach my human limitations.

I reject these first two choices for the third option. I believe that my soul is wholly connected with the eternal universe and the omnipotence of God. My mind seeks to operate in the infinite realm of my soul. What I can mentally conceive beyond the bounds of time and space, I believe that I have the power source to bring into reality--that is, to be experienced in the tangible physical world.

Through my soul I am spiritually joined as one with God. In this union I live not only with power but with a God-influenced set of values and standard of morality.

****

Reflect also on: FAITH, SOUL.

TIME

Time will manage itself; you must learn to fit your activities into its schedule.

As I complete this book, I am forty-four years and a hundred forty-two days into my life. That is, I have lived to use 16,213 days. Before giving it much thought, I would have said that most of my time was spent in school and on the job. It seems as though school and work are all that I have done. However, an estimation of the time actually spent doing these activities has revealed something different.

With a day being twenty-four hours (as opposed to an eight-hour school or work day) an estimated 1,200 days of my life were spent in elementary and secondary school. This is based on an average of twelve hours a day for getting ready for, traveling to and from, spending time in, and doing the home work for school. There were five days in the school week and forty weeks in the school year. I was in elementary, junior high, and high school for twelve years. I did not attend kindergarten. I traveled long distances to school to have available the resources for visually impaired students.

Allowing a generous sixty hours a week for attending classes and studying, only 630 full days were spent with college and law school studies. A year's studies consisted of thirty-six weeks.

I started working at my first full-time job at age twenty-five years. I have worked continuously for nineteen and three-eighths years. Only 2,325 full days were consumed by working. This is based on an estimate of 12 hours a day for commuting and working and an assumption of four weeks a year for holidays, vacations, and other leaves of absence.

So what have I done with the remaining 12,058 days (over thirty-three years) of my life? Sleeping an average of six hours a day, there went over eleven years. Watching television (or otherwise being entertained) an average of three hours a day, there went another five and a half years. But how do I account for the remaining approximately sixteen years?

Upon reflection:

As I pursue joy and success, time is my most valuable asset. When I run out of it, that will be the end of the whole matter. I cannot buy or work for more. No one can give me more time, and I cannot save it for later use.

Time is mine to use. If I do not use it now, I will lose it forever. I do not know how much I have available to me, nor is there a promise of any more than what I have already spent. Yet, I must plan to use tomorrow's allotment beneficially or it will be wasted.

Time is wasted when I spend it doing things that do not bring me joy or the desires of my heart. Playing, relaxing, or sleeping, for example, are not necessarily activities that waste time. Working on a job that I hate is a waste of my valuable life.

The fullness of life is not measured by longevity or endless activity. The gauge is the joy that I experience as I spend time doing what I desire and sharing life with others who, like me, seek the joy and fullness of life.

I will act now and for the rest of my life to make each moment full.

****

Reflect also on: HABIT, ORGANIZATION, PRIORITIES, PUNCTUALITY.

Thou wilt show me the path of life: in thy presence is fulness of joy; at thy right hand there are pleasures for evermore. [Psalms 16:11]

DAILY

READING

CALENDAR

A recommended reading calendar for you who wish to use this book as a source of daily inspiration.

JANUARY:

FEBRUARY:

MARCH:

APRIL:

MAY:

JUNE:

JULY:

AUGUST:

SEPTEMBER:

OCTOBER:

NOVEMBER:

DECEMBER:

Time will manage itself; you must learn to fit your activities into its schedule.

ALPHABETICAL INDEX

ABOUT THE AUTHOR

Dana LaMon is in his milieu when he writes to encourage, inspire, and motivate others. At age sixteen, he started giving inspirational speeches in his church. After he graduated from law school, both churches and schools benefitted from his presentations.

After his success in speech competition as a member of Toastmasters International, Dana started his business ImageWorth to motivate and enhance the self-image of others. With professional speaking as a supplementary business to his full-time job as an administrative law judge, his audiences include corporate and government managers, civil service and company employees, business owners and members of trade associations, religious congregations, prison inmates, and students from elementary school to college. His settings vary from the local classroom to international conventions.

Dana's personal experiences are exemplary of his message. People are inspired when they hear his words and note his accomplishments. He is a black man, reared in Compton, California, as one of twelve children. Despite his blindness at age four, he graduated from high school with honors, received a bachelor's degree in mathematics from Yale University, and earned a law degree from the University of Southern California.

After serving as the executive director of an independent living center for people with disabilities and maintaining a solo law practice, Dana became an Administrative Law Judge for the California Department of Social Services. He has served in that position since 1981.

Dana and his wife Jacqueline now reside in Lancaster, California, with their four children.

For information about the author's availability to speak, please call or write to:

ImageWorth
Publishing Division
P.O. Box 000
Lancaster, CA 93539

(800) 4-1-IMAGE (414-6243)

(To order additional copies of The Soul's Mirror, see the reverse side of this page.)

ORDER PROCEDURES

For a free catalog of inspirational and motivational products, including video and audio cassettes, call (800) 4-1-IMAGE.

Orders are placed by mail, telephone, or fax to:

ImageWorth
Publishing Division B2
P.O. Box 2117
Lancaster, CA 93539-2117

Tel: (800) 414-6243
Fax: (805) 942-7478

(PLEASE PRINT on a copy of this form or separate sheet.)

Name: ______________________________

Company, if any: ______________________________

Address: ______________________________

City/State/ZIP: ______________________________

Telephone: ______________________________

No. of copies: __________ X $24.95 = __________

Sales tax (CA orders only): $1.93 per book __________

Shipping: $3 for one book; $1, each additional __________

Total cost of order: __________

☐ Check/money order enclosed

☐ Charge the above total to my credit card
Acct.: ☐ AMEX ☐ CARTE BLANC ☐ DINERS CLUB
☐ DISCOVER ☐ MASTERCARD ☐ VISA

Name on acct.: ______________________________

Acct. No.: ____________________

Expiration date: ________________